ORANGE COUNTY HIGH SCHOOL OF THE ARTS

Masterpiece in the Making:
Composing OCHSA's First 20 Years

Santa Ana, California
www.ocsarts.net

Requests for such permission should be addressed to:
Narrative Development Corporation
231 S. Lakeview Ave
Placentia, CA 92870

Library of Congress Catalog Number Pending

Orange County High School of the Arts
Masterpiece in the Making:
Composing OCHSA's First 20 Years

ISBN 0-9776407-7-2-8

Printed in the United States of America

Edited by Gary Hernandez
Collected and compiled by Kate Peters and Doug Simao
Design and Layout by Anel Lopez-Cantu
Marketing by Jeanette Harvey and Cambria Morgan
Cover Design by Chris Liao, 12th grade, Visual Arts Conservatory
Photos and Illustrations by students and alumni of the Orange County High School of the Arts

www.ocsarts.net

Acknowledgments

In preparation for celebrating OCHSA's 20th Anniversary year, we embarked upon a project to collect as many OCHSA stories as possible. Our goal was to be able to use personal anecdotes to tell the story of the school at all major school events throughout 2007 and beyond. We knew that together those stories would tell the school's story better than any other kind of narrative. We collected stories from students, alums, faculty, staff, parents, and patrons, and anyone else with a good OCHSA story. We collected video taped interviews, as well as written stories. The stories were submitted to teachers as well as online via the OCHSA web site.

We are thankful to Dr. Ralph Opacic and everyone who took the vision of this book seriously and allowed us to use their stories and to all those who helped bring them together. We want to thank Sue Vaughn, the OCHSA Literature and Composition faculty, and all the Lit and Comp students for their help in creating and collecting the written student stories. We are grateful to John McMaster for helping us gather the online web submissions. Huge thanks go to Phil Rahn and the Film and Television Conservatory faculty for their help in scheduling and providing space for the video interviews, greeting interviewees and helping us understand the roles that people have played in the history of the school.

Once the stories were gathered, they needed to be typed and edited. We are grateful to Jeanette Harvey for overseeing this part of the project at OCHSA and also to Alicia Kozlowski, Kaitlyn Marriott, and Becky Parsons for their assistance.

Gary Hernandez was a natural choice for overall editing and we are grateful for his excellent work. Gary is also a great example of how OCHSA can inspire others. As he read the stories for editing, he began to contemplate the possibility of sending his own children to OCHSA, even though he lives in Chicago!

Cambria Morgan has been extremely supportive and helpful with this project from the beginning. We are grateful to Cambria especially for seeing the value and importance of this work and doing whatever she could to make it happen.

Anel Lopez-Cantu took the stories and the artwork and put it together in its final form, at which point the overall story came together as a work of art in itself. We are thankful for her very professional and artistic dedication to this book and to the story it tells.

We would also like to extend a gracious thank you to Jim Blaylock and Paige Oden, as well as the students and alumni of the Creative Writing and Visual Arts conservatory programs for submitting their works for inclusion in this book.

When we started this project, we knew that the story would be remarkable because the place is remarkable. This book is a testament to the school and to all the remarkable people who have created and sustained it. We hope that the book also serves as a reminder that dreams do come true when people believe in them and work hard to make them happen.

Sincerely,

Kate Peters and Doug Simao

Letter from John W. Daniels

Orange County High School of the Arts Foundation Chairman

Dear Friend,

The Orange County High School of the Arts is a premier, tuition-free public charter school that started out as one man's dream. Today, it is internationally recognized by prestigious arts and academic organizations. The story of how this dream came to be is remarkable, and includes people like you.

In this book, you will find an inspiring collection of stories told firsthand by the many people whose lives have been forever changed by the Orange County High School of the Arts. From students to alumni and faculty to community members, there's no doubt that the Orange County High School of the Arts has a magical effect on all those who pass through its doors.

I invite you, through the pages of this book, to become a part of this life-changing legacy and experience the wondrous effects of public arts education. Each story within this book is an essential part of what, when combined, becomes a masterpiece. May you find this in-depth look at one of the country's greatest arts schools as moving as those who have so generously contributed their personal stories to this anthology!

Regards,

John W. Daniels
Chairman, Orange County High School of the Arts Foundation

Letter from Ralph S. Opacic, Ed.D.

Orange County High School of the Arts Founder and Executive Director

Dear Friend,

As I reflect back on the past 20 years, I am reminded how truly amazing this journey has been. The story of how this dream came to be is remarkable and includes people like you. You believe not only in providing a quality education to our future generations, but also in providing a safe, challenging, and nurturing environment for our students to express themselves artistically.

Through the stories in this book, we celebrate the countless individuals who have made the Orange County High School of the Arts what it is today. As you read these individuals' stories, I invite you to become a part of the journey and join us as we look towards a future of continued success.

As we celebrate our 20th Anniversary season, I am honored and humbled by your continued generosity and support. I sincerely thank each and every one of you for your overwhelming support of our bright and talented students. Together, we continue to demonstrate our commitment to arts education and the next generation of world-class artists!

All good things,

Ralph S. Opacic, Ed.D.
Founder and Executive Director

Table of Contents

Table of Contents

Table of Contents

THE BEGINNING

"It was the best of times, it was the worst of times."

--A TALE OF TWO CITIES, BY CHARLES DICKENS

Photo by Michael Lucas, Visual Arts student

When we started with the concept of the high school of the arts it came out of my own personal experience coming here from Virginia trying to seek fame and fortune. All I knew was that I was somebody who was passionate about the arts and believed in it and there was no path for me; there was no mentor to take me there. It came out of my own personal struggles, so when we had the opportunity to create the high school of the arts that was the essence, the basis for why we created the school.

I certainly didn't know in 1987, when we started this, that we were one day going to be a school of 1,300, with the national and state recognition that we have. It was our dream to take kids, students that are passionate about the arts, and put them together with professional working artists and help those students find their way.

The OCHSA Story

♦

An Interview with
Ralph S. Opacic, Ed.D.
Founder and Executive Director

be whatever they wanted. Maybe that's what the vision sprung out of, but it sprung out of me being a teacher and wanting to impact the lives of young people.

Over the last twenty years, the Orange County High School of the Arts has gone through some difficult times. There was the battle in Los Alamitos as to whether we were going to be able to build OCHSA in Los Alamitos. There were moments when it would have been easy to give up and walk away, but I believed in what the Orange County High School of the Arts is, so much so that I was willing to fight on. When we came to Santa Ana, when we opened the school and the economy took a big decline, there was a battle to make sure we had the fiscal resources necessary to stay open. It would have been easy to walk away, but I chose to fight on. I chose to press on, believing we could get through.

When I started the high school of the arts, I was a high school music teacher. I just wanted kids to be as excited about singing and as excited about music as I was. Then when I had the opportunity to truly begin the high school of the arts, I wanted the students to be as excited about the arts, both the performing arts and the visual arts, as I was. I wanted to provide a path for them. I wanted them to see what the possibilities were in terms of pursuing their dreams. My goal was to teach these kids, to instill in them the belief that they could do and

The essence of the Orange County High School of the Arts is the teachers, the people. When we opened the new campus here in Santa Ana in 2000, David Greene and I wrote a song together. The lyrics go, "This place was made for dreamers and the dream begins today." We have been, and we still are, surrounded by artist teachers that have a dream and have created these extraordinary conservatory programs. We are surrounded by 1,300 students that have a dream of being artists. Despite facility limitations, despite financial

The OCHSA Story

limitations, we have been able to help these people find their way; we've been able to help these people accomplish those things, to build a bridge for them to that next place.

What is exciting for the future is the people are here—not only the teachers and the students, but those in the community who believe and support the program. The people are here; the program is here. We have a nationally-recognized academic program and a nationally-recognized arts program. The next and final piece is truly putting those resources in place—the facilities, the equipment, the guest artists, the master teachers—truly bringing together the resources so we can take these students and take them far beyond what we could imagine today.

I think one of the amazing byproducts we have created here, and again it wasn't anything we've planned, is that we've become a model. We've become a model of what's possible in arts education. We started the school back in the late 80's when school districts were cutting arts programs. Back then, the arts were in danger of becoming extinct. The high school of the arts was created, and then suddenly other Orange County school districts said, "Hey, if they are doing this, we better provide this service to our kids as well." So arts programs started popping up in other Orange County school districts. Huntington Beach Unified School District (imitation is the highest form of flattery) created a magnet school for their students in Huntington Beach. Capistrano Valley now has a magnet program. But it goes even broader than that; Riverside now has an arts school modeled af-

ter our program. In San Diego, Coronado High School has created an arts program modeled after our program as well. So what we have created here, the seeds we have planted, the foundation we've built, has been a launching pad for arts programs across the county.

Los Aangeles Unified School District has visited several times, and they are now in the process of building an arts school again, very much patterned after what we do here.

I feel like it's a responsibility. We're here in Orange County serving 1,300 kids and there are so many more students in Orange County and, of course, across California and the country that are hungry for an arts program. I almost feel it is our responsibility to invite those people to come and see the good things we're doing here. We're not competing with each other. We're raising and elevating the level of arts and arts education by being a role model, a model for those programs.

We've been a part of the International NETWORK for the Advancement of Arts Education for many years. When we started the high school of the arts, we became a part of that organization because we wanted to benchmark the best practices of arts schools across the country. It was a place where I could go, where other teachers could go to be revitalized, to be excited about the possibilities. Now twenty years later it is an amazing honor that the Orange County High School for the Arts has been named the International NETWORK for the Advancement of Arts Education's 2006 Exemplary School. We've learned from each other, we've

The OCHSA Story

taken the best from each other and turned it into something.

I think some people tend to forget that we are a public high school. This school is not my high school, it is not the high school of the teachers here, it is Orange County's high school, it is Southern California's high school. It's the cooperative work, the contributions, the dedication, the leadership of our staff of artist teachers, of our Foundation board members, our Trustees, and the community at large. The high school of the arts, in my mind, is the final piece of the puzzle of completing the arts and culture here in Orange County.

It's truly humbling to think about all of the people over the last twenty years who have committed their time, their energy, and their resources to make the high school of the arts possible. Especially in the last several years when school was struggling financially, people stepped up, people came in because they believed in the vision. And now it's amazing to me that we are continuing to build a family of people who believe and share the vision that is going to take us on into the next twenty years.

What's evident to me is that we have reached that tipping point. Our instructional program, our academics, our arts are being nationally-recognized. We have an extraordinary staff. We have amazing community leaders who believe in the vision, who believe in the school, who believe in the students, who want to help make it happen.

It's humbling and flattering when I am referred to as a visionary. The reality is, vision isn't much of anything unless you have the people who are willing to head down that path with you, who are willing to take a piece of that dream and make it their own, make it into something bigger and better. It's exciting to see that what we've started, the dream that started twenty years ago, has grown into what it is here today in Santa Ana. It is exciting to consider what the Orange County High School of the Arts is going to be in the next five, 10, 20 years. It's just humbling to be part of that journey.

It's funny. When the high school of the arts started I was single; I didn't have kids. I look back and I—you know the saying, ignorance is bliss—I just charged forward and figured it would all work out. Now that I have a family, now that I'm somewhat older and wiser, I realize what's critically important is getting up everyday and making choices based on what you truly believe. There have been some bad decisions, there have been some mistakes, but being willing to acknowledge those, being willing to learn from those, being willing to get up the next day and continue to focus on those good things that can be accomplished, that's what's important.

Character, integrity, trust: Those are the foundations upon which we have built the Orange County High School of the Arts. In our decision making, we must make sure we're always thinking of what's best for kids. We must treat each other with respect and dignity. We must celebrate each other's diversity. All of these things are a part of the culture we have tried to instill here in the last twenty years.

The OCHSA Story

At the end of the day, whether somebody becomes a famous singer or actor or musician, whether somebody's a successful artist or painter, whether somebody's a good teacher or a good administrator is not as important as whether they are a good person. Whether they are a person that is making the world a better place by who they are, by the way they treat each other, by the way they invest back into their community.

I see it in conservatory directors that have come here. I know very little about visual arts or film, but I know they capture the dream and then they turn it into something unique and special in that conservatory program. I have seen it in our school staff, our teachers. They go into that classroom equipped with innovation and a willingness and desire to connect with the kids. I see those parts, but I had never really thought of it in the context of when the students graduate from here whether we've developed dreamers, too.

If what we're accomplishing here is developing and graduating dreamers, we are doing a tremendous thing. The world needs more dreamers. It's the dreamers that are going to affect true change in the world. There's a quote that I hold onto that says, "Talent is hitting a target that no one else can hit, but true vision is hitting a target that no one else can see." We need more of those people that are out there shooting for a target that no one else can see or, even if they can't see that target, are willing to go after it.

A dream is meaningless unless you're willing to take some action and go after it. A dream is setting your sails to go in a specific direction. A dream is deciding to take a path and committing to that path because you believe that there is something better there at the end. A dream is a commitment to go on a journey, to go on a path as far as you can see and then having the courage to leap off into the unknown and having the faith that there at the end is something better.

I have always been surrounded by people that believe in me—my parents, my wonderful wife. I have always been surrounded by people who trust me. More importantly, I've always been surrounded by people who have not considered me to be a failure when I have made mistakes, but have allowed me to pick myself up, brush myself off, and press on.

I would hope that we do that for our students. Orange County High School of the Arts is an incubator. It is the place for them to explore, to experience, to make mistakes. At high school and junior high school age that's what growing up is all about, it's testing those things, testing who we believe we are; it's discovering ourselves through making mistakes. Again, aside from creating great artists, great performers, if we can help students discover themselves as people, who they are, and what talents they have aside from their artistic aptitude, then we will have been successful.

"The Kitesurfer"

By Alisha Vasquez
Creative Writing Conservatory Class of 2007

Opaque orange kite against a backdrop of blue

the shape of a moon sliver

the color of sunglow

Toes to heel

and toes to heel

in a chain of soft sand footprints

down the narrow peninsula,

the ocean like liquid turquoise

on both sides

white web of foam

on the surface

Body almost invisible

between so much blue

only a fragile link

between air and water

no gravity for a moment

only the pull of those four

diaphanous strings

circuitously up and into the clouds

THE HISTORY

*"When that April with his showers soote
The drought of March hath pierced to the root
And bathed every vein in such liqour
of which virtue engendered is the flower."*

--CANTERBURY TALES, GEOFFREY CHAUCER

Landscape by Aaron Vogel, Visual Arts alumnus

A Great Problem

An Interview with The Honorable Miguel Pulido
Mayor, City of Santa Ana

In the mid-1990's, my wife put a newspaper article in front of me which reported on the intense situation between Los Alamitos and the school district. I didn't really understand it, but they were talking about inter-district transfers. There was too much traffic. I thought, "Boy, what a good problem—to have a school that was so great that people were clambering to go to it. I don't understand why they're complaining." So, I reached out and contacted Ralph Opacic. We began a long series of meetings.

First we walked around the city to find a place that might work out. Frankly, we couldn't find anything. We then went around Fourth Street and saw small areas. He just said, "No, no, no, we need to think about something bigger." And I just kept saying, "No, no, no, you've got to come to Santa Ana." It all slowed down for a while, but then he came back a second time. About a year later we began talking in earnest.

The discussions became serious when I brought in Mike Harrah, a developer. I asked Mike if he would like to take one of these buildings and fill it with the Orange County High School of the Arts. Mike answered a question with a question and asked if they had the money. "No," I said, "they didn't have any money, but they will." I added that they couldn't get the money unless they had a building—but they couldn't get the building be-cause they didn't have any money. Clearly, somebody had to take the first step!

I have to give a lot of credit to a lot of people, but Mike Harrah deserves special credit because he took the leap. Let me explain, Mike started changing the building and working with the city to make sure it met the standards. Then we brought in the State. We worked diligently with the State architect and our own fire marshal to make sure the building was going to be safe. It was a long process, but in the end Mike had over 12 million dollars completely hanging—he had built the school with no contract or no assurance of payment. He just went and he modified this bank building to be able to accommodate the high school on a major leap of faith.

So we had a lot of long meetings to get the school to come out to Santa Ana. We started the trips. We started hosting people that came. The first folks we hosted were two board members. They were the true leaders; they were the parents, if you will, of the original OCHSA. I remember having them at my home and talking about what this meant: They were literally crying because they didn't want to let the Orange County High School of the Arts go, but the city was suing them and they had a lot of opposition internally. I said, "Look, you have to let it go free. It will become a more wonderful institution in the end. We'll be good hosts to the school."

A Great Problem

That was a traumatic few weeks, but they agreed. Then we started working with the staff, because this was a major undertaking. When they were in Los Alamitos, they had the portables and conservatories. The school was truly part of the Los Alamitos Unified School District. Here it was going to be a full charter, where the academics were also going to be part of what was going to take place within the school. We had to convince the unified in Santa Ana to allow this to happen. Keep in mind, they had never done this before. There were so many leaps of faith. People would say, "Ralph is great, the conservatory is great, but can he and the team do academics?" I would respond, "Yeah, they'll do great academics." And they'd say, "But how do you know?"

There were also folks who pointed out that we had to move 430 students—no easy task. There was also the fact that the state gave funding to the school based on the number of students attending. If the students didn't follow to Santa Ana, the school could lose everything. We needed money from the city to guarantee we wouldn't go flat if no kids came.

We ended up doing a redevelopment deal. We pledged and ultimately came through with 1.7 million dollars to cover the operational cost for a three-year period. When the move did happen, we went from 430 to 800 students! It all began to work out.

Now, it wasn't rosy overnight. Our money didn't come in all at once. Over time, though, we secured a three percent loan from the State of California through the treasurer for 20 million dollars. OCHSA then had the money to buy the building, to secure all the goodies inside, and to become operational.

When we started, we all thought it would be neat, we thought it would be cool. None of us had any idea the real impact it would have in so many real lives. Whenever I go to performances, or see anything affiliated with the Orange County High School of the Arts, I see a high level of commitment. I see kids who are happy doing what they're doing, kids who have found a home that nurtures their spirit. The students sacrifice so much to come here, and they feel so fortunate to be here. Here, in this location in Santa Ana that used to be a bank, in this location that so many people risked so much to make happen, in this location they have a true opportunity to develop into wonderful adults.

OCHSA isn't what it is because of a building— it's the vision, the community, the parents, the students. I'm not surprised about the National Blue Ribbon Award. I'm not surprised that OCHSA is one of the top schools in the country.

You're Lookin' at Him

An Interview with Mike Harrah
Caribou Industries

We met right after Ralph had lost his lease rights at the school in Los Alamitos. At that time he wasn't getting any help from anybody to reignite his school into another season. So I went and researched his school for awhile and checked out his location. I was amazed by the talent of the kids and the quality of the school. At the time everything was being run in trailers. It warmed my heart to see this type of thing going on in the world today where there are less and less places for people to send their kids for the arts. We met with Ralph and within six months we put together the entire school in Santa Ana as you see it today.

Miguel Pulido called me up one day and said he'd like to introduce me to Ralph Opacic, the director of the Orange County High School of the Arts in Los Alamitos. I met with him and showed him a couple properties. It was kind of funny. The first property I showed Ralph was 401 Civic Center. Ralph said, "This is perfect. I love this building." I said, "Well, Ralph this isn't it. I'm just showing you something that could work if this other one doesn't work for you." The building we ended up with works out perfect because it is almost a mirror image of the campus they had proposed to build somewhere else.

It was a lot of fun to work with Ralph. He was enthusiastic from the beginning. The city was also excited about putting things together. There was a money problem, though. Were there funds to build it? Who would build it? Who would finance it? Who would guarantee the loans? When I first met Ralph, he and Mike Ray came up to me and Walkie Ray.

They asked, "Who's going to build it?"

I said, "You're lookin' at him."

They asked, "Who's going to finance it?"

I said, "You're lookin' at him."

They asked, "Who's going to put the plans together and make it go and work with the city?"

I said, "You're lookin' at him."

They said, "Well, what we're looking at is a pretty tall order. Can you fill it?"

And I said, "Yes, and you're lookin' at him."

So I virtually put up my house and six other buildings I owned as collateral to get the loan, which was about $15.6 million to build the school. The risk was that if the school was not in session by September, the school would not have their grant from the state to repay me. We designed it, we built it, we put it together, and we had it open on time.

Unfortunately, during that period I got in a leeward wind sheer in a helicopter accident and broke my back. I operated and maintained all of the plans out of the hospital in rehab. I thank the Lord everything worked out and that I'm walking today.

Of all things, though, I am sincerely honored to have put together this school for OCHSA. It was worth every bit of effort. It truly is a fine school.

A Recipe for a Foundation
An Interview with Judy Sabbagh
Former Chairman and Founding Board Member,
Orange County High School of the Arts Foundation

Judy: I am Judy Sabbagh. I was the original chairman of the Orange County High School of the Arts Foundation. The school opened in the fall of 1987. Students actually applied in the spring and late summer and the regular school semester started in September of that year. The school had been started based on grants that had been written by school people, including Ralph, Dr. Jeanie Cross, and school board members at Los Alamitos High School.

Once the school started, the parents became involved. They approached several of the parents. There were only 87 students at the time, so it was an easy approach. Since my daughter was accepted to the school, I was one of those parents. There weren't that many of us; it was like an extended family. At the time when OCHSA first started it was a prerequisite that the students were from Los Alamitos High School in order to attend the High School of the Arts. Later on, they did accept students from outside of Los Alamitos High School for the after school programs. The Orange County High School of the Arts Foundation was established in 1988.

Interviewer: *What was your first impression of Ralph?*

Judy: He's so charismatic. Everybody involved was so eager to start the school, from the musical director to Ralph. Ralph had been a teacher, a music teacher and, therefore, his expertise was in the musical theater, which is what my daughter had applied for. At the time they only had a few departments: dance, musical theatre, technical theatre, and visual arts.

Interviewer: *What were some of the things you considered when you enrolled your daughter?*

Judy: We wanted to make sure the school was going to be substantial in giving

Photo by Evan Trine, Visual Arts alumnus

A Recipe for a Foundation

her everything that we had hoped for. We found that the school's plan was to conduct the musical theatre and the arts training after the academics portion of their school day. That was interesting to us. I've always likened the school to one-stop shopping. Although it would make for a long day, she would have all of her core classes in the morning and then the early afternoon. Then she would go on to dance, voice, whatever they were working on in musical theatre. They were doing productions as well, so that was exciting because at the time she was interested in pursuing that as a career.

Interviewer: *Well, not what you know now.*

Judy: The Foundation evolved from talking to my friends, talking to other parents who also had students there. The purpose was to raise money for the Orange County High School of the Arts. We were supposed to be self-sufficient. I ended up being on the Foundation board ten years; I was president for five years.

We would have meetings once a month. At the time there were about 15 to 20 of us. We would have phone-a-thons. One of the Foundation board members was a local realtor. She'd let us use her offices to call from, and Ralph would call as well. This was grass roots. Then, we decided we needed to do some other things, so we had the walk-a-thon.

We would meet and decide how we could involve everybody to continue to raise money, but it was very basic compared to what they do now. The Gala started out to be the OCHSA auction, Hearts for the Arts, the very first one. We held it at the Disneyland Hotel, and not in the grand ballroom.

Interviewer: *Can you recount one of the more memorable events?*

Judy: One occurred when we decided that we were going to have a recognition

A Recipe for a Foundation

of the students and of the Foundation, members who had worked so hard to raise money. The event evolved into the Season Finale. That was in the second year. It was incredible how we got the attendance there. At first we only asked five dollars to attend, but even then the parents didn't want to pay for that extra performance, so that was always a big challenge.

But I'll never forget the first Season Finale when the air conditioning wasn't working. We've got Lew and Margie Webb, who had been the benefactors from the get go, and we were just sweating but the kids performed well.

I met Lew and Margie Webb in Kenya, Africa in 1987. We were at the Mount Canyon Safari Club. Courtney and I were having dinner getting to know the people on the tour. My younger daughter, Courtney, is fairly loud. She said that her sister, Stacey, was going to apply for the Orange County High School of the Arts. Well, Lew and Margie Webb were sitting like an earshot from us. Margie, who is just the most gracious southern lady in the whole world, gets up and says, "I don't mean to be forward, however, did you say the Orange County High School of the Arts?"

I said, "Yes." And she said, "Oh, well, they named the performing arts center after me." It was because Lew and Margie contributed a certain amount to refurbish what had been the cafeteria at Los Al High School. So that's how we first met.

Interviewer: *So what was it like to work with them?*

Judy: They are extremely gracious people. Their children were grown and gone, but they had such a passion for Los Alamitos and the arts. Lew wanted to have something named after Margie, which was quite altruistic. They were heavily involved from a financial standpoint, and they cared so much. They were always at performances even though they lived in Laguna Niguel, which is no short drive. They donated items for us to

A Recipe for a Foundation

auction off, things like a lease of a Lexus for a year, and they hosted many fundraisers at their home in Laguna. They were so down to earth. They're just fabulous.

Interviewer: *What was the most rewarding thing the financial help was able to fund?*

Judy: The most rewarding thing in my estimation has been to make the Orange County High School of the Arts a public school and enable bright and talented students to be able to attend without having to pay tuition. To see those students develop their talent in an environment that is so nurturing without having to worry about paying for it has been deeply gratifying. Think of the talent that might have been overlooked or undeveloped if many of those kids couldn't afford to come to OCHSA.

Interviewer: *Is there a special message you would like to give to Ralph?*

Judy: Ralph, it has been a journey. We know in our hearts that this school has meant everything to both of us. I found that throughout the years you were always focused, you were always there not only for the students but for the people that needed to support the school. Your dedication has been unwavering.

We've all come a long way, the school especially. Who could have envisioned from 1987 with the 87 or 88 students that there would be the number that there is now? But equally as important, it's the family that's been created by the Orange County High School of the Arts. And whatever paths the students choose to take, they will always be a part of that family.

A Gift of Love

An Interview with Lewis and Margaret Webb

Founding Board Members and Long-time Supporters,
Orange County High School of the Arts Foundation
Community Partner, Orange County High School of the Arts Foundation Advisory Board

Lewis and Margaret Webb started out with OCHSA when it was just a dream in Ralph's mind. They have been with the school ever since. They've seen the school grow and mature and the students along with it.

Lewis: The school board Superintendent in Los Alamitos was Chuck McCauley. I was in a Rotary Club with him. One day Chuck turned to me and said, "Lew, we're going to try to get a school of the arts started within the high school framework at Los Alamitos, a school within a school. But we need some financial help—we'd like to convert the multi-purpose room in the school to a theater. Could you see fit to help out and take a naming opportunity, maybe the Lew and Margie Webb Theater?" I said, "Let me think about it. I really don't have an interest in the naming for myself, but maybe for Margie, because she's always known as my wife, Karen's mother, Jeremy's mother." And so I thought it over.

I saw Chuck the next week at Rotary Club and said, "Chuck, I think I'd like to do that for Christmas for Margaret. I've gotten her everything in the world for Christmas, but I never got her a theater." We laughed and talked about it. I followed, supplying the financing to convert the multi-purpose room to a theater room and stage.

Margaret: I was an only child, so I was always the Stafford's daughter. Then I was married young, and, as he said, I was Lew's wife. Then we had a late child after, well, our other kids were 16 and 19 when Jeremy came along. When he was born they put up a huge sign on the high school saying, Jeremy Webb, born six pounds, so many ounces. And I thought, "Wow, here we go again! I'm Jeremy's mother now!" Which is wonderful, and I've loved just being a mother and a wife. I just thought I never aspired to anything grand, other than being a mother and a wife. And that's what I had devoted my life to doing, and hopefully doing it well.

Lewis: Ralph constantly asked me to come by and take a look with him and approve things that were going on. I didn't need to approve them; he certainly knew what he was doing—he did a masterful job. It was a fantastic auditorium and stage. It was the Margaret A. Webb Performing Arts Center. As we were walking from the car, and Margaret saw that, she turned and buried her face in my chest, almost as if she was embarrassed by it. I always enjoy looking up and seeing that on the building when we go to performances.

A Gift of Love

Margaret: To have a building dedicated to me was not something that I had ever considered. It was thrilling, and it remains thrilling, to have been given that gift of love from my husband. Every time we go to a performance, we're tickled that my name is on the theater and that we're a part of it, a part of the kids being there. The thrill of having a gift in my name is incomparable. Anybody can do it if they just make a donation, small or large, in someone's name to the school.

Lewis: Then there was a time when the school couldn't stay at Los Alamitos. I was involved in trying to help Ralph make a decision to relocate. I was sure that we were going to build in Los Alamitos. As it happened, we went in an entirely new direction. The deciding factor was a traffic problem that just couldn't be mitigated. It was a sad thing to see. I thought that was the end, but Ralph seized that and went with it and consequently the school still exists today.

Where will it go? I envision the growth of OCHSA to be colossal. I think it will be recognized throughout the United States as a center for young people to perfect their arts.

Photo by Kurtis Kennington, Visual Arts alumnus

Education First

An Interview with William Lee

Member, Orange County High School of the Arts Foundation Board of Directors

William: My name is William Lee. I currently serve on the Foundation Board of Directors and am vice president of the Support Group Committee. Prior to that, I served on the school's Foundation Board of Trustees. I am the proud parent of two OCHSA graduates. My daughter graduated the last year at Los Alamitos. My son graduated the first year here at the Santa Ana campus.

Interviewer: *Your son knew he was coming here before you did. What was that like?*

William: We were working with the parent groups and the students over at Los Alamitos about coming to the Santa Ana campus. I was one of the parent leaders in the Commercial Dance Conservatory. I was busy working with Ralph and with the parents trying to decide how we would best present the Santa Ana campus. One day Ralph came to me and said, "Congratulations, Robert's made the decision to come to the Santa Ana campus." I had actually heard it from Ralph before I heard it from my son, which is a tribute to Ralph. It shows how much my son thought of the school and of Dr. Opacic.

Interviewer: *What was it like being a parent when your daughter was at Los Alamitos? Was it different than the Santa Ana OCHSA?*

William: I don't think the experience between the two schools was that much different. My daughter had wanted to go to OCHSA when it was on the Los Alamitos campus. We had a home in Los Alamitos, so we knew of the high school's academic reputation. The real driving force for her, however, was the Orange County High School of the Arts, the OCHSA experience. She was one of those students who tried out as a freshman and didn't make it, tried out as a sophomore and didn't make it, tried out as a junior and did make it. She then got incredibly busy those last two years to try to work her way through and become an accomplished commercial dancer. My son Robert started out as a freshman in the program immediately and transitioned over to Santa Ana in his senior year. I didn't see a big difference. It was a little longer of a drive, but the core program—the academ-

26

ics, the arts, the continuity of the program—have been fantastic between the two.

Interviewer: *So did you begin working with OCHSA when your daughter was accepted, or were you involved before?*

William: We knew of OCHSA before my daughter was accepted. We had some friends of ours whose daughter had gone here, and she spoke highly of the program. We actually attended many of the OCHSA programs and commercial dance performances because she invited us to see her.

My two children went to a dance studio in the area and heard of OCHSA there. One of the great stories for us as a family is that one of the first people my son came in contact with was David Sidoni. He was one of the master teachers at his studio and, of course, he had graduated from OCHSA. There were connections all over the place; it just seemed a natural for our kids to attend the school.

Interviewer: *So your daughter was not accepted the first time or second time she applied. Tell me about the first audition that didn't work out.*

William: She worked exceptionally hard. She wanted to get in. Her studio dance program started later for her. She was in the 11- to 12-year-old range as opposed to the six-year-old range. So she worked hard, but didn't make it. Rather than being defeated, she became more energized and worked even harder for another year. She tried out her sophomore year, but, again, didn't make it. And again she became more determined. By the time she got in her junior year, we were nervous. We were hoping and praying that she would make it because she put so much energy into it. She did quite well on her own. She actually injured herself playing soccer, as I recall, and was having some difficulty during the auditions. According to the director, however, she had made it in the first auditions. So it was well worth the time and the effort for her. As parents we enjoyed how the director handled the whole audition process and encouraged the kids to continue to come back. It was a good evolution for her.

Education First

Interviewer: *What is your daughter doing now?*

William: When Michelle graduated she went on to Chapman University. She was originally going to major in dance. She wanted to work in the area of special programs with children who did not get the chance to experience dance the way she had experienced it. When she was in school she transitioned her interests and switched her major to psychology, with a minor in dance. She surprised all of us when she announced in her master's level training that she was going to become a credentialed teacher. Michelle started teaching this year after having completed her masters and teaching credential at the education school at Chapman.

Interviewer: *You have been a big supporter of OCHSA. What is it about OCHSA that makes it something that you want to support?*

William: One of the first things you see as you come into the school is the diversity of the student population. The second thing you notice is that diversity is focused on eleven different disciplines, each student being passionate about whether they are in musical theatre or whether they are in film and television or whether they're in commercial dance or classical dance. It is immensely rewarding to see kids so passionate about the arts and at the same time remaining focused on academics; to see the academic level so high, the artistic level so high, the passion so high; to see these students getting along so well and to be so accepting of each other. When you go into a regular school, you don't see that. When I was in high school, being both a band kid and a choir kid, I struggled for acceptance. Acceptance is the key aspect of OCHSA. It's an energy that's so immense and so real; you it feel when you come through the door.

Interviewer: *Let's talk about your son's experience. He also graduated from OCHSA. Tell us his story.*

William: Robert entered the program as a freshman in the Commercial Dance Conservatory. He branched out while he was here. He left commercial dance and actually went into the production group, spending some time there as well augmenting his dance training with outside training from master

teachers. He returned to commercial dance in his junior and senior year. While he was a junior and senior, he also was working professionally. That was difficult to do. It's difficult for the school; it's difficult for the students. You have to do your homework before you leave, and you have to take the test the minute you walk back into the program. The academic teachers, the arts teachers, the administration all worked together to make sure that this student, who had this passion and this ability at such a young age to get out and work professionally, could do just that.

He works today professionally. As well as being a dancer, he is a choreographer. He has acted as well. All of those accomplishments were predicated on the experiences he received from attending OCHSA.

Interviewer: *What kind of work does he do as a dancer?*

William: Robert works as a commercial dancer. He is on tour with artists from time to time. He dances in the commercial market for advertisements, with the music awards shows, and music videos. He has danced behind Celine Dion at awards shows and he did a Pepsi commercial with Britney Spears. He danced with Jodi Messina in her first live country TV appearance, which was a special thing for him, as well as for her. He is on tour right now with Cheyenne, traveling internationally in South America, Mexico, and Puerto Rico. He went on tour with a dance troop and was able to see portions of Europe, including Germany, Austria, and Switzerland. So his experience out there in commercial dance has been extremely diverse.

Interviewer: *Is there anything that you would like to say that you haven't said already?*

William: I am extremely pleased with the Orange County High School of the Arts on many different levels. My experience is not only as a parent, but as a parent volunteer. My experience has been as a Foundation board member in support of the school and as a parent in a social environment with other parents. There are so many levels at the Orange County High School of the Arts where a parent and a student have an opportunity to engage, to enjoy, and to celebrate not just the arts, but also to celebrate their children and other parents' children. It's a wonderful community. It is a unique community and may well be one of the few communities like it in the United States, maybe even the world.

Interviewer: *I know you are particularly involved with the alums. If we were to do an appeal to the alums to be involved in some way, what would you say to them?*

William: My father just passed away about three weeks ago, and it makes me a little bit reflective. The one thing that my dad said to me as I grew up, and I am now fifty years old, was that if you had the opportunity to do something that was your avocation and it became your vocation, consider yourself fortunate. OCHSA gives that opportunity to student after student after student. The second thing my father always challenged me to do was to return something back to the community. I searched and searched most of my life trying to figure out what that meant. If I was going to do that, exactly how was I going to do it?

I have been fortunate as a parent to be given the opportunity to put something back into OCHSA, to thank them for what they provided for my students. I hope that one day the students themselves who have benefited by it will have a rekindling of their passion. I hope they come to recognize that whether they chose a business or an arts career, a lot of who they are and the success they enjoy come from what they learned at OCHSA. I hope that someday they will be in a position, like I am, to be able to return to OCHSA and to be able to help the school solidify its legacy. Then, at some point, we can all look back, whether it's 10 years, 20 years, 30 years from now and know that this institution will never go away and that we, the parents and the students, have been instrumental in somehow endowing this institution and protecting it against the budget pratfalls that inevitably come as governments shift year in and year out, as new congressmen and new senators and new governors come in, and as priorities shift, that this institution will be insulated forever from those pressures of government.

Landscape by Lydia Kung, Visual Arts alumna

Education First

Interviewer: *For the building campaign: Why is it important to expand this campus?*

William: The development of the Orange County High School of the Arts campus for the future is important so that current and future students get the opportunity to experience things students ten years ago didn't. Technology changes and the professional environment changes, so the school needs to be able to adapt to those changes for the sake of the students.

If you stay in a building and you allow that building to get old, you have a bit of a legacy, an antique. A lot of folks appreciate an antique. I think young students appreciate more than antiques: they want to see a live, virulent school. In business there is the adage that if you don't grow, you wither. I don't think it's that much different in the education business and we want to make sure that this school continues to grow.

Interviewer: *Why Santa Ana?*

William: When I drove into Southern California many years ago as a northern California kid, there was a water tower in Santa Ana that read, "education first." I had no idea what Santa Ana was like or what they meant by "education first." I happened to buy my home in Los Alamitos and I still didn't know what "education first" meant. When OCHSA needed a home, when it was quite possible that OCHSA would wither and die because Los Alamitos did not have the room for us anymore, when Santa Ana worked so hard to recognize what OCHSA was and bring us here, it lived into the definition of "education first." When the mayor worked so hard to get us here, when private developers worked so hard to get us here, when people for no reason other than the fact they wanted OCHSA to be here worked so hard to get us here, why would we want to be anyplace else? Santa Ana's "education first" slogan on that water tower years and years ago and the current Santa Ana focus on arts—If that doesn't define OCHSA, nothing else does.

The First Day in Santa Ana

An Interview with Kelly Ruggirello

Former Vice President of Development, Public Relations & Marketing, OCHSA Foundation

The staff arrived early with great anxiety and anticipation and excitement. If you build it, will they come? Getting ready, we took a moment to reflect on all of the hard work and the time and the money that it had taken to get to this place and all of the people who made it possible. Ralph's management style doesn't allow failure, so we never discussed not being able to do it. We always discussed how we were going to do it, when we were going to do it, how we were going to fund it. But it was right. When something's right and you know that it's meant to be and it's the right move for the school and for the students and for the city—when everything is in line, it's just a matter of how to make it work, not whether it's going to work. It was never a question for us.

We all waited outside eager to see the first cars pull up, the first students dropped off. We waited just to watch them walk onto the campus. The students appreciated it, I know, having facilities that were worthy of them, as did the faculty. We had always been facility poor and program rich. Now we finally had facilities that showed respect for the talent we were recruiting. It was a magnanimous moment to have those students come onto this beautiful, new campus built just for them.

It was as life-changing moment to experience all of those feelings in one moment as the doors opened and the kids came through. It sounds like a simple concept, but egress and ingress issues were very real. Getting everybody to go up the stairs and down the stairs and play well with others in the staircase—all of that made it exciting and heartfelt.

I think the best part about that day was it was easy for them, it was natural. We made it an easy transition for them and they were thrilled to be in a vertical campus which doesn't happen in California unless you're a charter school. At that moment everybody felt special to be here on this campus. While few remember all the hard work, time, and money it took to create this campus so quickly, it is incredibly fulfilling to know that we helped make the dream a reality.

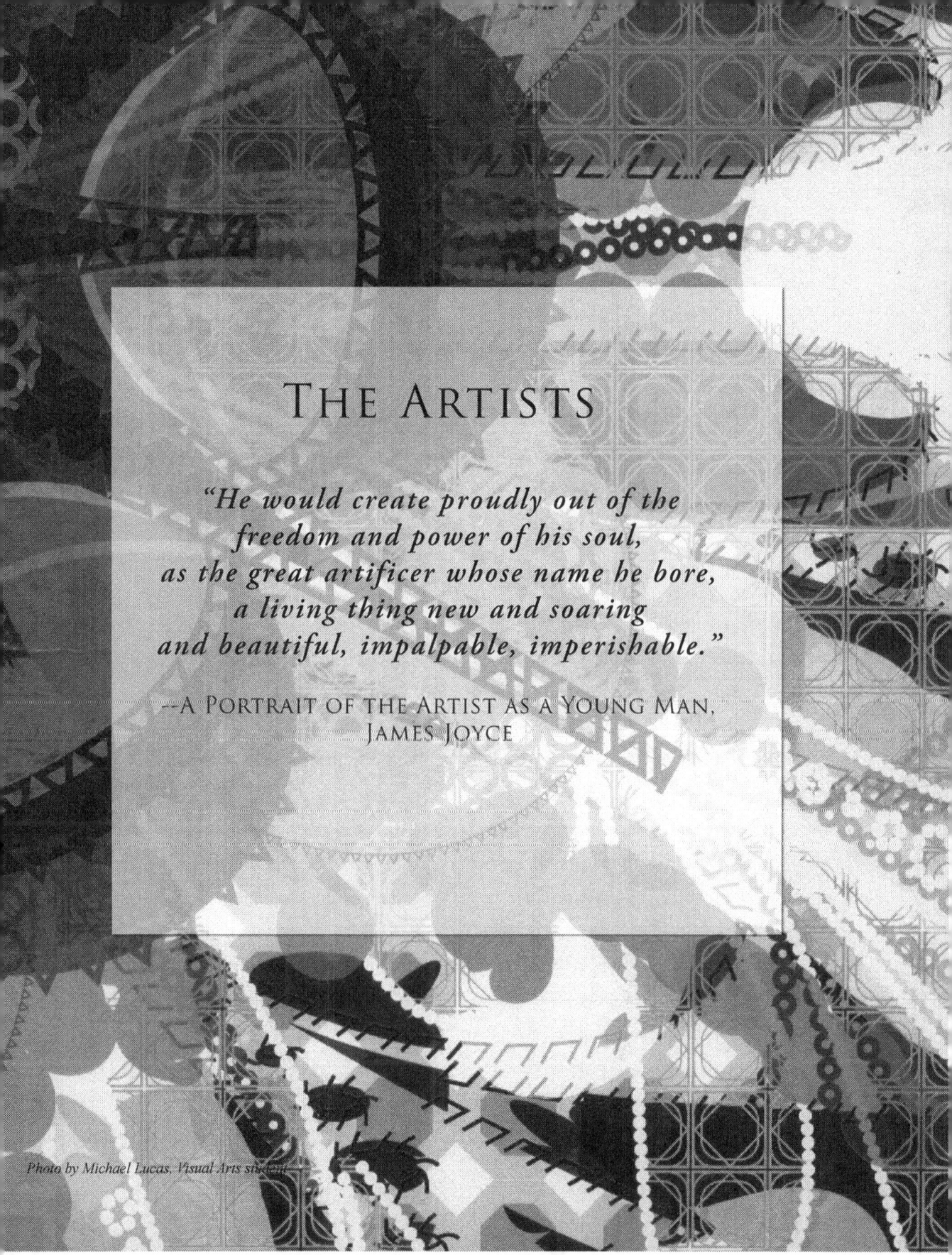

THE ARTISTS

*"He would create proudly out of the
freedom and power of his soul,
as the great artificer whose name he bore,
a living thing new and soaring
and beautiful, impalpable, imperishable."*

--A PORTRAIT OF THE ARTIST AS A YOUNG MAN,
JAMES JOYCE

Photo by Michael Lucas, Visual Arts student

Elevator Pass and The Principal Actor

An Interview with Barbara O'Connor
Artistic Director and Founding Principal

Elevator Pass

We have only two elevators on our campus and the kids always want to sneak on the elevator, so discipline at the school consists mostly of elevator referrals. You can see how difficult life is here!

Students can obtain a bona fide elevator pass for medical reasons. A particular young lady had such a pass because she was unable to walk up and down the stairs. One day I got on the elevator, chatting with some students. When they got off, I noticed I was left alone in the elevator with six backpacks. So, I picked them all up and dragged them back to my office. I figured the students would come looking for them and they'd have to explain how I ended up with all of their backpacks.

As it turned out, this eighth grade student had taken it upon herself to create her own elevator pass system through which the students would pay her to transport their backpacks because they didn't want to carry them upstairs, even though it may be only one flight. She would record what floor the student wanted his/her backpack delivered to. She'd say, "You want to be left off at floor three?" Out goes the backpack—and so it

went: floor five, floor six, floor seven. She would throw out backpacks on each floor according to her ledger and, as scheduled, the students would retrieve their backpacks. Quite the efficient and lucrative operation.

I have to admit I commended her for being so creative. Originally, no one said it was against the rules. So now we've had to tell the students that it's inappropriate to make money with such an endeavor and that it is against the rules. But, I was secretly delighted at the level of entrepreneurship!

The Principal Actor

The school's *Art Attack Live,* which is a daily student-produced news show, gives students the opportunity to appear on camera. I don't particularly like being on camera, but a couple of years ago the students running *Art Attack* told me that I needed to be on the show along with the students

I pleaded, "Don't make me; I don't want to. That's what you guys do. That's not what I do." As a compromise, we worked out this system in which I would stand just off-set and talk into a little microphone.

Elevator Pass and The Principal Actor

I would be off-camera, but the kids could hear me reading announcements.

Unbeknownst to me, the students directing *Art Attack* had created a puppet kind of person to represent me. I think Conan O'Brien does it, or maybe it's Jay Leno. They create a caricature or puppet to represent someone and the puppet's mouth moves as the person speaks. I went on *Art Attack* and the students made the "mini me" look different every day. They added my glasses and then constructed jewelry and different outfits . . . and kept my lips moving! I am told the funniest one was when they had me in a bikini—I think it was the body of Britney Spears. Someone finally clued me in to what they were doing. I have since given up and now go live on camera. "Mini me" has retired.

Barbara O' Connor joined Orange County High School of the Arts as principal in 2000 and was responsible for the planning and development of the school's outstanding academic program. As Artistic Director, she currently oversees the development of the instructional program for the school's eleven arts conservatories. O'Connor has served as an educator for over 30 years for students from Kindergarten through college in Orange County.

A Voice Like Honey

By Michelle Tymich

Music and Theatre Conservatory Class of 2007

Music has been a part of my life ever since I can remember. In pre-school, I took Yamaha keyboard lessons every other day. From then on, I played the piano. Music has always been around me. My mom played an Elton John song on the piano which she learned when she was ten years old. It's the only thing that she ever learned on the piano, but she still knows it today. That is a really amazing thing.

Throughout my life, I have tried many different activities. I ice-skated, did ballet, played basketball, practiced Tae Kwon Do, and I even tried cheer-leading. I did all of these thinking that there could possibly be something I wanted to do other than play the piano. On April 27, 2003, I realized there was something of the sort. Rabbi Cohen explained to me, after I read my haftorah, that my "voice was like honey." I was blown away with her words. I never gave my voice a chance. I was an athlete, I didn't sing. Shortly after my Bat Mitzvah, my grandma enrolled me in voice lessons with an eighty-six-year-old woman in Long Beach.

Ever since that day, I have grown. There is something else other than playing the piano that I can call my own. Music is what makes me who I am, and if I hadn't started with those Yamaha keyboard lessons, I would probably still be searching for what makes me special. I decided to apply to OCHSA my sophomore year of high school. I was accepted into the voice department of the Music and Theatre Conservatory.

OCHSA helped me become even more of what makes me "me." It brought to my attention who I am not, and that is totally okay. It's important to know who we're not, as well as who we are. I'm not an athlete, I'm a musician, and I like the sound of that.

The Art of Life

By Alan Yu

Visual Arts Conservatory Class of 2007

I have often wondered whether life imitates art or art imitates life. Was my life guided by art, or did art guide my life? When I reflect upon turning points in my life, one event in particular seems to illustrate the perplexity of this question.

It was a chilly morning in January when my parents officially announced that they weren't going to send me back to Fairmont Private Prep Academy the coming fall. I was in sixth grade at the time, and I had been to Fairmont since preschool. I met my best friends during my seven years there. The announcement wasn't terribly shocking, because we had previously talked about leaving Fairmont. My parents wanted me to experience the world more fully, and through our discussions we decided the Roxbury Latin School in Massachusetts best fit my needs.

The second part of their announcement, however, was terribly shocking. They told me I wasn't going to Roxbury Latin School but rather to Cerro Villa Middle School, the public junior high of Villa Park. Through my friends, I heard of the atrocities that occurred there such as water bottle fights at lunch. Cerro Villa had a tightly knit social hierarchy that consisted of mean, obnoxious, spoiled, and conceited kids. Hence, I was quite apprehensive to go there.

Later in May, I went onto the campus of Cerro Villa to register for next semester. Registration was right after school, so I was still in my Fairmont uniform. As I walked down the slick marble halls of Cerro Villa, people gave me dirty looks. In one glance they evaluated who I was based on how I looked. Wearing a Fairmont uniform violated the first unspoken rule of being a Villa Park local. It demonstrated a disregard for city and school pride. As the smallest city in Orange County at 2.1 square miles, Villa Park had an overwhelming sense of community and spirit. My heart sank as I realized I would be spending the coming fall at the bottom of the food chain at a school known for being obnoxious.

After registration, I went home feeling pessimistic. Later that night, I received a phone call from my friend Phyllis who exclaimed, "Alan! I'm not going to Fairmont next year either! I'm going to be a visual artist at OCHSA!"

The phone call was the beginning of what Dr. Opacic would call "salvation." A spark went off in my mind as I asked her what OCHSA was, where it was, and how I could register. In my mind there was no comparison between Cerro Villa and OCHSA. Phyllis had described OCHSA with vivid details as a safe haven for artistic expression. I always had a passion for the arts from a young age and I had assembled an extensive portfolio of ceramics and oil paintings by the age of twelve.

Photo by Mary Amor, Visual Arts alumna

The Art of Life

There was no question in my mind that this school would be the perfect alternative to Cerro Villa, so I proceeded to call OCHSA the following morning to request a registration packet. As luck would have it, I obtained the last visual arts audition slot offered for the following school year.

It would be easy to say that OCHSA was the first day of the rest of my life and that through my art classes I found true beauty in the world and a reason to live. Such is not the case. The answer to my fundamental question is that life dictates arts and not vice versa. Art cannot dictate life; therefore, life cannot imitate art. Art is unreasonable.

It does not meet any of the basic needs of survival. Furthermore, art is irrational. A reason or purpose does not have to exist for the creation of art. In essence, it is merely entertainment. Life is structured, and thus to entertain the thought of art being able to dictate life is frivolous. As a result, living life is the foundation for all art. And it is only when a person begins to live that he or she can begin to grasp the beauty and art in this world.

The Best of the Best

By Matthew Craig
Music and Theatre Conservatory Class of 2006

A nine-year-old sticks out like a sore thumb on a high school campus. It's September 15, 1998. I was going to visit the most renowned arts high school in Southern California and the place that would later turn out to be where I would spend seventh through twelfth grade—the Orange County High School of the Arts, otherwise known as OCHSA. As I walked in and out of classrooms, I saw people performing monologues, doing scene work, practicing improv, and singing; all things that I was familiar with and enjoyed above all else. When I left that day, I knew OCHSA was the place for me. Theatre was, and continues to be, my passion in life.

In sixth grade, I attended Oak Middle School in Los Alamitos and was on track to go to OCHSA in Los Alamitos when I reached high school. But then something great happened. OCHSA relocated to Santa Ana and became its own independent charter school. The even better part about it was that it also included a middle school. Nothing better had ever happened to me. I immediately called the school to submit my grades for the next year and schedule an audition date. They must have been surprised to hear an 11-year-old kid asking to submit his own grades! But, they did tell me that they would begin accepting applications in March. Sure enough, come March I submitted an application and was given an audition date. My spirits soared.

OCHSA accepts only the best of the best. Now that I look back on it, I realize I was not the best of the best at the time. I'd say I was in the top 25 percent, but not any farther up. My first few years in the Music and Theatre Conservatory were rough sometimes. Some of the other students had recording contracts and were doing professional shows in Los Angeles and New York. I was a Southern California-bred community theatre boy. I would sometimes feel intimidated by the other students because they were so darn good. They would never make fun of me or be unfriendly in any way, but everyone knew I had the most to learn of all the people in the group. As the years went by, I became better and better. I started landing better roles outside of OCHSA and some me-

The Best of the Best

dium-sized roles in the school shows. Last year, I had the most important role in the ensemble of *Cabaret,* our school wide production. It was fantastic! Not many juniors get such an opportunity. Through unrelenting resolve and sheer determination to succeed, I brought myself to the level of all of the other students at OCHSA and beyond.

When I wake up in the morning, I don't always have a cheerful disposition and I am not always ready in time to beat the traffic. But one thing holds steadfast, I look forward to going to school and seeing all the people I have come to love over the past six years. I can go to school with a smile on my face and a positive attitude to get me through the long day. Good things are always in store for me at OCHSA; this is a fact. All of my teachers are serious about what they do and expect excellence from their students at all times. OCHSA is not for the faint-hearted. The school is demanding and will test one's resilience. The faculty wants to know you are serious, and once they know you are serious, you will become great.

When I go to college, I want to bring some of that hard-working attitude to my classes.

The standards that have been instilled in me at OCHSA, beginning when I was in seventh grade, are those of the professional world. College sounds exciting to me, and it is something I want to do. I can bring to college an unwavering work ethic and a love of theatre like no other. What I want to do with my life is to be successful in theatre. I am willing to put forth my best effort in order to achieve that goal. College will be a stepping stone to the next phase of my life, a theatre life. The next four years will not be easy, and I don't want them to be. I want to be challenged at every corner, take the hardest classes, and go to the auditions that I have no chance at. College will provide that for me and will put me on track to becoming all that I can be, and more.

I will never stray from my course, never lose focus, and never give in. These are the values of life and theatre that are the most important to me. These are the values I will bring to college and uphold for the rest of my life.

One Crooked Chronicle

By Megan J. Frazier

Classical and Contemporary Dance Conservatory Class of 2008

As a child, nothing was as important to me as growing up to be a prima ballerina. In the year of 1994, also known as the early stages of my life, my mother took me to my first ballet class. Dressed in pink tights, a pink leotard, pink ballet slippers, and with my hair tightly fastened in a bun, I looked like a bottle of Pepto-Bismol hopping around in a dance studio.

During those lessons, my mother would watch in the window and smile as I twirled around. She would hide around the corner to make sure I didn't see her watching, but I knew she was there supporting everything I did. Ballet was my life. Nothing stood in the way of my dreams of being a dancer. The only worries ever to cross my mind concerned completing three pirouettes out of thirty-two fouettés on stage. My life was planned out for me. I was going to be a principal dancer in the American Ballet Theatre.

Coming to OCHSA was no struggle for me at all. Being the advanced dancer that I was at the age of ten, I was confident that I would be selected in the Classical and Contemporary Dance Conservatory. My background of dancing at Ballet Pacifica, under the teachings of Gillian Finley, and rigorous training at ABT summer intensives was enough to guarantee my spot. I knew I belonged at an arts school. I knew I needed to be with other motivated students who aspired to be great artists as well. And sure enough, I was selected as a seventh grader to participate in classical dance. I was one step closer to my dream.

As the years passed, I grew. No longer the four-foot, ten-inch individual that I was, I grew to be five foot, seven inches. Along with this growth spurt, I developed scoliosis. This, in turn, changed my life forever. Being that my entire life I had enjoyably watched the Discovery Science and Discovery Health Channel, I was well aware that I had an abnormal lateral curvature in my spine. I knew that it was not as severe as other children's scoliosis, but it took a toll in my dancing ability. The curvature of my spine changed the anatomy of my feet, making pointe dancing extremely painful and difficult. My balance was impaired, my range in movement was altered, and my back ached. Soon, my enjoyment in dance reduced to the point of pure hatred. I wanted to be a physician, not a ballet dancer.

In the summer of 2004, I attended an ABT Summer Intensive at UCI. At this time I received a Charleston Bending Brace from my orthopedic surgeon to prevent any more curvature to my spine. In case you do not know, the back brace is

Sketch by Caitlin Knox, Visual Arts alumna

One Crooked Chronicle

a gigantic, plastic corset to be worn at night that leads to insomnia not to mention humiliation at the hands of your siblings. That summer the brace caused injury to my spine, ending any satisfaction in dance that I had left. At that point, my life took a turn for the better. My dream and ultimate goal in life was now to be a physician. To cure those in pain, as I felt from scoliosis, and to do what I loved, which was to study and practice medicine.

In 2005, I transferred out of the Classical Dance Conservatory into the Commercial Dance Conservatory. The summer prior to the fall semester, I met a girl named Chloe. In a jazz dance class I noticed a girl in front of me with a scar down her back. I asked her what it was. She told me her life story of having scoliosis and surgery to correct the curve by using metal rods. What was amazing was her love for dance and still continuing to dance after the doctors told her she would never walk again. Chloe changed my life and propelled me into going into commercial dance, which is what I love. I love dance that involves expression. I love the freedom of movement in that style of dance. And what I love most is the satisfaction I receive from my dance classes, which now allows me to be a happier and more successful academic student.

This year I attended an NYLF seminar on Medicine at UCLA to direct me to my goal of being a physician. At this seminar, I attended multi-ple plenary sessions and heard from some of the world's leading physicians. I heard from a man who is curing the world from AIDS. I spoke with a pediatrician who is saving the lives of children with diabetes. I was able to visit my dream college, USC's Keck Medical School, and speak with amazing physicians and professors. I know now that being a doctor is my purpose in life. To cure others who need help is what I am here to do.

Yes, dance will always be my form of self-expression and creativity, but I am most thankful for dance because it brought me to where I am today. It has made me a performer onstage and in society. And I will continue dancing for as long as I can. OCHSA has also shaped me into who I am today. It has allowed me to experience two dance forms and has supported me with every decision that I have made. I now know that no matter what happens to me in the future, I will do what I enjoy most. Because, as Confucius is credited for saying, "Choose a job you love, and you will never have to work a day in your life." And who knows? That little four-year-old ballerina could soon grow up to be a leading physician in the world of medicine.

An Alternative Way of Dressing

By Rosalind Millson
Visual Arts Conservatory Class of 2008

I have walked through the streets with my friends and have heard mutterings such as, "Are they hippies?" or "renaissance people." Not only does that make me proud to realize that my friends and I are, perhaps, a little different than the average teenager, but it also brings back haunting memories of pre-OCHSA days. I can picture a small, brown- haired girl blending into the mass of jeans and Billabong t-shirts. The only way I was different to them was that as they took notes, I was concentrating on sketching the teacher.

On my first day at OCHSA, I dangerously bumped into a girl with cat ears and jet-black hair. To my surprise, there was an evident lack of jeans and t-shirts. I observed long, flowing skirts, brightly mismatched colors, and, to my horror, mismatched shoes. The next day, I wore a bright pink t-shirt with orange pants. I had realized that there was an alternative way of dressing, and, to my great joy, an alternative way of thinking. All my fellow students had opinions and were not just a mass of students; they were individuals. This is something I wanted. I had always had my opinions and beliefs, but they had always somehow blended with the general consensus.

Did this mean I now had to start backing up my beliefs and challenging them? Yes, if I had any chance of keeping them. I began to research my claims, listening to other people's perspectives, and questioning everything I was told. I now had a standard to live up to and could not let individuals that filled my classrooms down.

Although my dress sense has somewhat calmed down, my opinions are strong and steady and backed up with research and evidence. I am challenged everyday at OCHSA, and I am ready for debate. I look forward to the future, and the many individuals I have yet to meet. OCHSA has instilled in me, through the diversity that fills the halls and classrooms, a new perspective of life and the many facets that one might view it with.

On Finding Comfort

By Julie Shendelman
Creative Writing Conservatory Class of 2007

In the weeks leading up to my first day of freshman year at my traditional high school, I plotted. I sat on my sofa, sketching pictures of girls with dark, long hair, corsets, too much eyeliner, and pants that had too many straps to count. She was the ideal Hot Topic girl, the girl I strived to be. After years of high ponytails, short shorts, and glitter, it was time to recreate my look.

September arrived quickly. I strolled out of my house with black swirls painted on my cheek and freshly dyed red hair falling over my shoulders. My pants jingled, each strap smacking against my legs as I went. My best friend since kindergarten didn't even recognize me as I scaled the steps in front of the school. In true high school fashion, I was instantly dumped; we were never close again.

After choir, I went on to Geometry. There I made my first friend. She sulked into the classroom a couple minutes after I did. She scanned the room nervously, her black hair flowing in my imagined breeze. She spotted my pants, almost exactly the same as her own, and plunked down next to me. I went on to make more Hot Topic friends.

In order to keep up appearances I started writing poetry. My new best friend carried a notebook with more than a hundred sheets of paper in it. Each sheet had a handwritten poem. She showed me her work. It was terrible, but the sheer quantity of her pieces overwhelmed me. I was competing now. The first poem took a long time. This was taken straight out of my freshman year journal:

How can alone be so small a word,
When it fills every aspect of life.
When some are long, they are truly alone.
The silence can cut like a knife.

But when I'm alone, I feel less lonely,
than when I'm with us, them, and we.
And when I'm alone, I never am lonely,
because I know that I'll always have me.

Tragically, it was the best poem I had ever written. I wanted to show everyone. Instead, in math class the next day, I folded a note with my verses scribbled inside and passed it to my friend. I saw her smile at the paper and scribble a response. There, in her bubbly handwriting was the result of my anguish. "Why is it so perky? LOL." Frustrated, but determined to impress her, I decided to dig deeper.

I went on to write my second poem. It started like this:

So much to say
so much to tell
not confiding in you
is like being in hell.

Apparently, my idea of hell was a world

On Finding Comfort

where one had to solve one's own problems. My friend wasn't allowed to see this one. Acknowledging that my poetic skills were lacking, I decided to perfect my craft before letting anyone see my work. I went on to write nearly fifty poems, most of which were as terrible as the first. Slowly, they started to improve. But at the same time, I was growing up less and less happy. At school I was teased for dressing "darkly." I stopped returning my friends' calls and gave up on dating.

In the summer between freshman and sophomore year, my phone stopped ringing altogether. My friends were so busy I got a job. When I wasn't working, I was writing. My poetry was getting more angst-ridden each day. I wrote on scraps of paper at the restaurant. When I got home, I would empty the pockets of my apron. Crumpled napkins and receipts floated onto my bedroom floor, fresh poems for my journal. Work turned out to be another place where I didn't fit in; the waitresses were a large part of my high school's "in-crowd." I was ignored when I spoke. I quit the job when school started up again.

I toned down the wannabe Goth look. I was tired of being mistreated because of a pair of pants and some black makeup. My hair was still dark, but my bondage pants were collecting dust in my bottom drawer. I rediscovered the glory that was, and still continues to be, denim. I also started to call myself bisexual, in an attempt to fit in with all my friends.

After a few months of muddling through

a rocky relationship with a girl, I came out of the closet as a lesbian to my friends and family. All of my friends were surprised. By the end of the year they were "over it" and called themselves straight again. I did the exact opposite. I knew, even then, that my true self was starting to form.

I kept writing. I wrote the first few pages of my first story, "Sahara." I never finished it. The same thing happened with the stories that followed. "Trapped" and "Black Crayons" got lost under piles of homework, unfinished.

I put some distance between my old friends and me. School was starting to feel like a dead end. Two of my friends went to an alternative high school for those in danger of dropping out. I was lonely, and it showed in my grades. I had no motivation to do homework or even stay awake during class.

One weekend my Jewish youth group took everyone to camp. I didn't have many friends there, but I was overjoyed at the chance to spend a weekend away. During a group activity, I struck up a conversation with a girl. As it turned out, she was an OCHSA student. I had no idea that the school had a creative writing program. I was intrigued, but forgot about our conversation and enjoyed the rest of the weekend.

A couple of months passed. It was about the third quarter when I found myself at my saddest. I desperately wanted to get away. Being gay was not easy at my school. A year before, a girl had tried to come out of the closet. People started

Photo by Evan Trine, Visual Arts alumnus

On Finding Comfort

to send her threatening text messages. They said terrible things to her and put her through terrible abuse. That summer she killed herself. I was constantly worried that something would happen to me. Fortunately, I managed to avoid any hate crimes, though I received my share of rude comments.

It felt that no matter what I did, I was still being misjudged. Now known as "the lesbian," it seemed no one saw any other aspect of me. I started to evaluate my options. Graduating early was impossible—my grades were hardly good enough to skip a year. It was then when I remembered my conversation with the girl at youth group camp so many months before. It wasn't long before I was filling out an application to OCHSA.

I spent the next two weeks digging through my old poems, refurbishing and perfecting them. Everything went in—the best of my poetry and essays I had written for school, pages of my writing, paper clipped to a series of forms. I slipped them into a big envelope and sealed it. I knew OCHSA would be my only chance to break free. The next morning I slid the envelope into the mailbox. I had trouble focusing for the rest of the day and the days that followed.

A few weeks later I was talking to my friend Brian about an upcoming chemistry test. He had just started to explain something about molecules when my cell phone rang. My mom asked me where I was and when I was coming home. I asked if I could stay a little longer to finish talking to Brian.

Mom paused for a second. "Are you sure you want to wait? There's a letter here." I was silent. "It's from OCHSA." I screamed that I'd be home in a couple of minutes, said goodbye to my friend and ran into the street, barely dodging a car. I was out of breath when I got home. My mom and dad stood silently as I tore open the envelope. Registration information. I cried.

After that, things started looking up. I made friends on the first day at OCHSA. My grades skyrocketed almost instantly. It turns out that being happy does wonders for a student's motivation. I learned not to hide who I am out of fear of being judged. Also, my writing improved. I gave up the five-paragraph essay and the rhyming poem, though I did learn meter for fun when I want to rhyme. I also read my poetry for an audience for the first time. The adrenaline rush was incredible. I finished my first story, then my second, and then my third. After writing almost twenty, I decided to be a writer.

I'm so grateful for the direction and confidence that OCHSA has given me. With college approaching so quickly, it's good to know that I'll be ready for whatever comes my way. But more importantly, I'm grateful to have the freedom to be original without judgment, to be creative without limitations, to finally learn to be myself.

Fateful Trace, Saving Grace

By Rachel Bres
Visual Arts Conservatory Student Class of 2008

I sat on the edge of Grammy's bed and immersed myself in her coffee table book on cave art. My six-year-old mind ignored everything but the large pictures in the book. The light changing through the window and illuminating the dancing particles floating through the air usually possessed my interest, yet even that was forgotten as I peeked through the book. I felt guilty as I investigated the first few pages. I did not want the cave people to see my interest as an intrusion on their lives, yet as the page numbers increased and remaining pages lessened, I grew to know the ancient work as if it were my own.

Bulls were their specialty, I deduced, for they commanded much of the wet, grey walls upon which the artists sketched. Staring at the book, I felt a connection. It was not a relational connection, yet one much deeper. I knew the artists, and they knew me, for I realized we had art in common. I stopped flipping the thick pages and started at one cave scene. There was a man chasing a bull with a rugged spear in hand. I could draw that, I told myself. As any young and interested artist would, I placed my crisp, white paper on top of the book and sat under the forest green lamp that lit Grammy's dark room. I picked up a pencil, sharp, as she always kept them—she was a published author, after all—and started to lightly outline the caveman.

He appeared to be too meek, so I repeated my action seven times until he was at the desired color, a distinguished grey. I picked up the paper and held it away from me. As I looked down at the book, I realized that I had made an indentation on the caveman. I slowly felt the page. Guilt fell upon me like crumbling rocks. I was convinced that I had ruined the art, the ancient art! I carefully closed the book, rubbed any fingerprints off of the shiny cover, and walked quickly to Grammy. I glanced over my shoulder, as if protecting myself from the cavemen. When I finally reached her, I opened the book to the fateful page and showed her. I pointed to the marks and hung my head. She was silent for a time, and then spoke.

"Rachel, this is the cave man's only way of survival."

I was convinced that she did not understand that I was silently attempting to admit my fault, so I motioned again, and her reply was unexpected.

"Dear, people make mistakes, yet it is how they survive through their mistakes and hard times that save them. How will you be saved?"

I looked up at her face carved by wisdom, sadness, and experience, and deduced that maybe indentations did not ruin things after all.

After the full moon rose over the rough roofs of houses in her neighborhood, I left with my mother and sister. I glanced back at her house, confusion brewing inside of me. Her silhouette was framed by a dim light, and the moon shone down on her face. I turned away and found the cratered moon in the sky. He winked at me. He understood what I could not.

Fateful Trace, Saving Grace

Years elapsed since the incident, and OCHSA jumped into my life. I created my art, considering only what was taught to me by the influential teachers, and forgot the past.

After an exciting mid-September day at school, I was informed by my mother that Grammy was gone. I reeled back from her embrace and slowly retreated to my room. I sat on my bed until my pale window framed darkness—and the moon. I stared at His full face and He sympathized with me. I fell asleep with Him watching over me.

I was awakened by my dad, and he whispered to me that I would not be going to school today because we would be going to San Diego to sort through Grammy's belongings.

The car ride was longer than usual, and the silence blistered my heart. Not the silence in the car, but the silence that I felt inside of me. I had not been prompted to draw since the day I heard of her departure. For a reason I could not identify, I had automatically carried my sketchbook with me, although I had no intention of utilizing its beckoning pages. It rode on my lap for the entire trip to her house. As we parked at our destination, I slowly exited the car. The sketchbook fell open to an unfinished sketch of Grammy and me, smiling. It occurred to me that my depiction of her was incorrect, yet I did not know how to fix her. My mother called for me to go into the house with them, so I carefully closed my sketchbook, set it on my seat, and trudged up the concrete stairs leading to her house.

Grammy's room was dustier than it used to be, yet it still smelled of books, her passion. Her walls were lined with them. We used to refer to her house as the "mini library," for that is what it was, a library. My sister, Rebecca, and I sat to sift through her excess books, stacked on the ground, for there was no more space on the walls to fit them. At the bottom of a large stack, one book was familiar to me. It was a coffee table book, *the* coffee table book that prompted her intuitive words to me.

I dusted the cover with my sleeve to make it as shiny as I had remembered. I opened the cover, acknowledging the welcoming crack of a book that had not been read in many years, and flipped through the pages. Anticipation was building up inside of me, and yes, there it was—the page with the caveman holding the spear and chasing the bull . . . and the indentations. The night of her clandestine response swelled into my mind. I experienced a sad realization, for I realized of what she spoke. I grabbed the book, ran down the stairs, and jumped into the unlocked car. My sketchbook was waiting for me; Grammy was waiting for me. I found the page that consisted of our happy faces. I reached out for my unsharpened pencil and filled in her face with wrinkles, wrinkles of wisdom, sadness, and experience.

During my next weeks at OCHSA, I experienced a growth in my art. I was not restricted to the apparent; I depicted what I felt inside. I was inspired by Grammy's words. I had survived through my trial—and my savior was art.

Owning the Entire School

By Savannah Rigley
Creative Writing Conservatory Class of 2007

I am abrasive—straight up, even. I am confident, compassionate, and fair, just to name a few.

Madame Friederichsen, my French IV teacher, says that in order to fully harness the French language, you have to "own it." I think that personalities are the same way. If you're confident, then own it. If you're funny, make it an art form. If you're ugly, wear that badge with pride.

Writing, this one is for sure, is the exact same way. Ms. Carr, when not talking about James Joyce, says the following, "There should be more concrete details in this poem." She is referring to the poem in front of us.

"No," I say, like the bigheaded senior that I am. "Keep it vague." I scratch my head, "Well, I guess, it could go either way. But in either case, you have to take it wildly one way or the other." In other words, *own it.*

Writing is like that. There are no rules. The only rule is there are no rules. Well, that and please, for the love of God, do *not* use the words, "scream," "darkness," or "razor suicide" anywhere within your piece. Trust me.

In elementary school my teacher said, "The ONLY way to write an essay is to include five paragraphs, each with blah blah blah blah." I am paraphrasing because I know you have already heard this spiel.

In high school, a senior last year informed junior-me that "five paragraph essays are bull and those essays are useless and blah blah blah blah."

Pop Quiz: What do the above two people have in common?

Answer: They are both wrong.
Write any way you please. Here is where the disclaimers begin. Keep with me. It gets good later, I promise. I was making a gross generalization earlier. Writing, if it has taught me anything, has taught me that while there are no rules and nobody, I mean *nobody,* can tell you what to do, sometimes you *are* wrong. I admit, I am not often wrong, but sometimes I am. And when I'm wrong, it can be in a big way.

Now wait, says the educated reader. You aren't making any sense. How exactly do I know when I'm being wrong? Easy-peasy, says I. Open your ears to criticism and to the wise words of your peers and elders.

"I want to *see* wind blowing in your hair. I want to *feel* the worry when your fingertips graze the man running in front of you. Don't tell me you're scared he'll leave, *show* me," says Ms. Carr.

The seniors in the back of the class nod sagely. "There are certain things you want to watch out for," I tell her. "For example, don't just list adjectives to tell me what you're thinking. If it's a four letter adjective, it better not be on its own line."

Painting by Natalie Oleinik, Visual Arts student

Owning the Entire School

Fast forward a day. I'm sitting in another class with a different teacher. A girl across the room says in a ridiculously obnoxious voice, "I want to SEE your hands reaching out for HIM! I want to FEEL it, class! FEEL IT!" She screams this last part and the teacher looks up. "I hope you aren't making fun of me." "No," I tell him. "I know who she's making fun of."

I tilt my head toward her, frowning. She smiles and says, "Eat me."

There are a million rude things I could have said to her. But I didn't. I don't regret helping her with her poem. And I don't feel any need to follow that up. The knowledge that she will never learn to be a better writer if she doesn't listen to the advice of those around her is comfort enough.

There are three lessons in that last anecdote. First, of course, is take your criticism well. In writing, you will get rejected twenty times for every one story you sell. The second is know when to stop. There was no need to engage in a fight with her. It wasn't worth it.

The third, and perhaps most vital, is, simply, own it. The confidence required to be creative and give creative feedback is the most important thing I've learned from my creative writing teachers. Some people told Gertrude Stein she was a hack. But, her "Identity: A Poem" is one of the most beautiful pieces of experimental writing I've ever read. Plenty of people probably informed Shakespeare that his tragic heroes were all wrong and that his plays had too many acts.

This may seem contradictory. How is the above girl wrong and William Carlos Williams right for ignoring the naysayer? Owning it is *not* trying to elevate yourself above others by cutting them down. Owning it is having the courage to take your criticisms and incorporate them into something better, to listen to my elementary school teacher, and that senior, and realize there's a happy medium. There's more than one way to do things. *Every* good writer has an editor. Every. Single. One. Nobody's first draft is brilliance. Not Stephen King, not Flannery O'Connor, not Raymond Carver. And I can guarantee you that John Updike doesn't mock his editors over lunch with his friends.

OCHSA has taught me these valuable lessons. I have the confidence to raise my hand in poetry class and tell freshmen my learned wisdom from years of writing bad poetry and being wrong. I've transformed from an insecure eighth grader to a confident senior who calls people on walking up the wrong side of the stairs. I've mastered it. I've turned egotism into an art form.

I love me. I wouldn't want to be anybody but me. However, when my teachers, who have gone through a lot more schooling that I have, or my peers, tell me that perhaps "screaming razor suicide" was *not* my best work, I can own it. I wrote it and I thought it was good, but I can see where they're coming from and maybe it does need a new title.

Most importantly, I have the confidence, courage, and integrity to say it to their faces. I own my opinions. And I'd be happy to hear yours. I'm honest, and sometimes I can be a little abrasive, but I'm fair, compassionate, and straight up awesome.

A Passion for Dancing

An Interview with Malia Simonini
Ballet Folklorico Conservatory Class of 2007

My mom put me in Ballet Folklorico when I was four. She thought it would be good for me because, as she said, I had way too much energy. So, I started dancing when I was four and I'm still at it today. I absolutely love it. When I was in fifth grade, I took a year off of dancing. It was the worst year of my life. Afterwards, we looked into a group here in Santa Ana. In total, I've been in four dance groups.

When I was in sixth or seventh grade I wanted to come to OCHSA for music and theatre. At the time, they didn't have ballet folklorico. My dad came and checked out the campus. He felt it was too open for me and that I was too young.

When I finished junior high my mom and dad told me that OCHSA had added a new conservatory, ballet folklorico. It seemed interesting, so I looked into it. I looked into the academics as well as what the conservatory was going to bring into the school. I liked what I saw, so I auditioned. I made it in. I love the school, I love the curriculum, and I love my conservatory.

I recently tried out for a professional company in Santa Monica—Ballet Folklorico Pacifico. They dance at the Ford every year and go to China and New York for competitions. It's more ballet, more projections. I've never done that kind of ballet folklorico before, but because of the curriculum at OCHSA, I was able to make it into the company.

Free to Be Me

By Danica Kennedy

Commercial Dance Conservatory Class of 2009

This is my fourth year attending OCHSA in the Commercial Dance Conservatory, and I love it here! There are many people that share the same joys and passions, and it is fun because you can be yourself without worrying about what other people think. I enjoy being in commercial dance because I get the chance to perform frequently and be with my friends. Personally, I am a social person and I have a lot of friends that have interesting and unique qualities.

Before I came to OCHSA I attended a small private school and went to dance class afterwards. I remember my first day at OCHSA. I saw a lot of exotically dressed up people dancing and singing while going through the hallways to their classes. I thought that was so weird, but now I know that people are just expressing themselves and having fun. Now I don't even notice people like that anymore because I am so used to it.

Now that I go to OCHSA, I get the chance to practice my craft as a serious major, instead of just an extracurricular activity. I learn more about dance while attending OCHSA. There are a lot of opportunities given, which can possibly help me in a future career. There is a really positive attitude at OCHSA because almost everyone has goals and dreams they are trying to achieve. My favorite thing here is the freedom allowed in areas such as thoughts, opinions, personalities, ideas, friends, and style.

I have learned a lot from OCHSA. Now I have a different approach to everything. Through my conservatory I have been able to meet famous choreographers such as Brian Friedman and Nick Lazzarini, both of whom have inspired my style of dance. I am never afraid to be myself, and I never worry about people judging me. I have enjoyed meeting many talented people who are truly amazing at their art form. It has changed my life. I love it!

I Am a Menopausal Woman, Metaphorically Speaking

Anonymous

Yes, now that you ask, there is something I would like you to know: I have had an early-life crisis. I know what you're thinking. Crises are reserved for forty-five-year-old housewives wondering where their youths went, and for fifty-something accountants contemplating "What does it all mean?" But yes, at age sixteen, I experienced a legitimate crisis. Rather than dropping my life savings on a butternut squash convertible Porsche, or dropping nine carbohydrate laden pounds, a la my middle-aged counterparts, I dropped traditional school in search of a new alternative. (Gasp.)

And let me tell you, I'm no slacker. I've been a hit-the-books-no-time-for-play kid, achieving straight A's since the first semester of fourth grade when I repulsed myself after receiving my first and only "C." But that over-achiever mentality wore me out. Eventually, years of two o'clock bedtimes, solid honors and advanced placement classes, homework-packed weekends, and anxiety-ridden days began to take a toll. I was tired. I was unhappy. And I did question where my youth went, and I did ask myself, "What does it all mean?" And I realized it was time to make a change.

So I did. Instead of returning to my academically

I Am a Menopausal Woman, Metaphorically Speaking

pressured private Jewish school, where not only regular academics but also five years of Hebrew and Judaic Studies proved exhausting, I retained a home school teacher. I completed all credits necessary for winter semester of my junior year, and eventually transferred to the Orange County High School of the Arts (OCHSA) during the spring semester of my junior year. At OCHSA, I resumed taking rigorous classes, both academic and film, throughout the course of a nine-hour school day. I also involved myself in student organizations. But more importantly, I achieved a balance.

You must be quite bored hearing about "finding inner peace," and "surmounting obstacles." Millions of kids do it. It's quite common. The fact that it is so common leads me to believe that balance is the most important quality of life, and I strive to maintain that balance.

Of course there are extremes residing on both sides of the student spectrum. Imagine a student so immersed in schoolwork that she can't even picture herself having fun. Class occupies the day; homework consumes the night. Tests, essays, reports, book work—it never ends. She works herself into a pathetic sobbing frenzy just staring at the day's work schedule. Her heart palpitates at the mere mention of a pop quiz.

And on the other end of the spectrum, imagine the "student" who doesn't care if she fails; it's "all cool," she responds nonchalantly to her nagging teacher regarding her late assignment. She chooses the beach over a study session and has never set foot inside of a library. Sometimes she completes her work, usually in twenty minutes.

The former describes the student I used to be. The latter describes the classmate I envied. But there is a happy medium, and I have discovered it. I can overachieve while being happy! I study, but I also spend time with friends and family, take dance classes, make films, and write creatively. I still feel that drive to succeed and I am still a high energy individual; however, I now focus my energy on being content with myself and my work, not my transcript. I am psychologically healthier. True, I'm not yet ready to put my obsessive-compulsive nature to rest. Nevertheless, my early-life crisis allowed me the opportunity to take a critical look at my life, and actually find ways to improve it. And God knows, self improvement is the most trying task on the average adolescent's "to do" list.

"The Poet"

By Sarah Horn

Creative Writing Conservatory Class of 2010

She rides the bus,

her rain coat slick with

water and mud, her

notebook full of dreams

clutched to her chest.

She's sick of filing paperwork,

sick of having a worthless passion,

sick of her writing being both

a puppy on the foot of her bed

and a bulldog that won't let go.

She could be the poet laureate

and she'd still have to work

at an insurance company to make ends meet.

She's smart enough to be anything,

but she chose to be a poet,

to be the voice for a mute world.

It is her burden, her struggle,

her comfort and her light.

THE PLACE

"In Xanadu did Kubla Khan
A stately pleasure-dome decree:
Where Alph, the sacred river, ran
Through caverns measureless to man."

--KUBLA KHAN, OR A VISION IN A DREAM.
A FRAGMENT,
SAMUEL TAYLOR COOLRIDGE

You Could Never Truly Understand

By Justin Gubersky

Music and Theatre Conservatory Class of 2007

"I don't understand what's so special about a school with crazy artistic kids." I was told this repeatedly before I came to this school—by teachers, parents, and some of my old friends. I didn't really understand it either. I came to OCHSA without any expectations of it being that different from any other school. A tall bank turned into a school. I had no idea how much one place could affect and shape so much of who I am. It has not only shaped me artistically and academically, but has made me a better person.

Starting off, I figured I would get used to it. But there is always so much happening here. Once I finished adjusting to one way, I have to shift to another. For almost six years I have had the opportunity to meet so many people and teachers who have greatly influenced me—six years of incredible people with incredible artistic ability, six years of classes that change every year, six years of climbing up and down stairs.

Coming to this school was like jumping into a moving car. And my attempts at trying, at first, didn't go so well. The first day I walked up those stairs I was brimming with excitement at the thought of the potential ahead of me. I started to walk up those long stairs, but before I could make it halfway up a flight, I fell flat on my face. People just kept moving around me as I sat on the stairs.

Finally, one girl helped me up. All she said was, "First day?" I nodded. She laughed. She then continued up the stairs; a great way to start off my first day at a new school. But I would fall a lot here, and somehow there has always been a person to help me up.

I was faced with many challenges and I am grateful for each one. My teachers challenge me to have an open mind. For example, in my acting classes we would do exercises that challenged our emotions, which helped us not to act but "to be real under imaginary circumstances." Sometimes the exercises challenged us so much that people would leave the classroom crying. People would then begin to stare and think, "What did the teacher do to you?" Then all the people crying would just start laughing because they reached something that was real to them, but not real in relation to reality. To us, we were arguing about our heavily sick father at his house. In reality, we were on the second floor of OCHSA. I know I never could have accomplished anything like that at any other school.

I was shocked that my counselor knew my name the first day I walked into her office with a question. Part of it probably had to do with the incredible resemblance to my brother, but she never forgot it. And somehow she still manages to remember everyone's name. I and many of the staff

You Could Never Truly Understand

members had never seen someone that committed. So much of what I have done at OCHSA has made me a better person, physically, mentally, and artistically.

I remember going outside at the beginning of this school year and seeing my friend with a huge grin on her face, something that I had not seen in a long time. I sat down next to her on the curb of Tenth Street and said, "What are you smiling about?"

She responded, "I'm going to miss *this*."

Confused, I asked, "What do you mean miss this?"

She said reflectively, "All of this."

Looking out at the school I have had the pleasure to attend, I do not know how I am going to leave this seven story building, this church turned into a theater, all of the people I have met, and all of the memories I have had on every one of those seven floors. I'm going to miss always being surprised and having unexpected things occur. The first day of school this year, I saw a girl who tripped on the stairs and fell down.

I helped her up and said, "First day?"

She responded, "No, I've been going to this school for three years and I'm never going to get used to these stairs."

OCHSA has meant so much to me and someone who hasn't attended the school could not understand my experiences. Standing with a spotlight beaming on my face, discussing existentialism in one class and getting to perform it in another, being able to sit at a bonfire with the friends that I have met there, my teacher giving me twenty minutes to memorize a specific monologue and then perform it in front of the class. I have been given such a secure environment to let me take risks, make mistakes, and succeed. To me, that's something that can never be replaced.

So when people say, "I don't understand what's so special about a school with crazy artistic kids," I'm not denying we're crazy. I'm sure there aren't many schools where people can break out in song with three part harmony, or sketch a drawing they could sell to an art gallery, or scratch an idea down on a napkin and easily get it published. With so many differences and such diversity, this has created something common between all of us. If that's not special, I just say, "You could never truly understand."

Just Like Coming Home

An Interview with Patti Stern
OCHSA Parent and ENCORE! Member

ENCORE! is an auxiliary membership organization created for patrons of the arts who wholeheartedly support the school's mission. ENCORE! offers current parents, alumni parents, and community members the opportunity to socialize with others who are passionate about arts education and interested in supporting the next generation of world-class artists.

I was a part of the original group that formed Fanfare, one of the school's support groups. Fanfare's mission was to raise community awareness and funds for OCHSA. At that time, we were just people in the community, very few parents, that saw the benefits of the school for the entire community. Then, Fanfare slowly evolved into what is now ENCORE!, which presently is primarily parent-driven. I stayed on the board because I fell in love with OCHSA. I don't think I ever had any intention of leaving after that first year. I felt like OCHSA was truly coming home, but it was even better than home. OCHSA was like going to heaven. For the students that are fortunate enough to be accepted into these programs, I really do think they've arrived at an artist's nirvana.

I know, because I was an art kid, that it's hard if you don't have outlets into which to funnel your creative energy. It can be difficult. It sounds esoteric, but it's real. Artistic kids need to do what they need to do, and OCHSA gives them that op-portunity. I especially like the fact that they get to glean experiences from so many different communities and counties. There are kids coming here from San Diego. A friend of mine who is down in San Diego had a daughter who rode the train up to Santa Ana for four years.

Upon graduation, the students go off to wonderful colleges. While at OCHSA, the students cultivate a professional presence that allows them to be successful in whatever field they choose. It just feels good being involved with OCHSA. I sound like a cheerleader, but that's what it does for me. There's a lot of warm fuzziness that comes with being involved with such an amazing institution.

The first time I walked the halls of OCHSA, I fell in love with the school. If you peek in, you'll hear students singing in one room, playing piano in another, and dancing in another. It's exhilarating. Also, I've watched, in the six years since they've come here to Santa Ana, phenomenal growth in the school in all areas. The kids are happy here. You walk on this campus and never feel like anyone has a gun to their head at 7:00 a.m. when they are leaving home. As a former art teacher, it would be heaven to teach kids who wanted to be in school everyday to just soak up what the teachers were putting out there.

Jump into the Mystery – Ben Vereen

By Alexis Sweeney

Music and Theatre Conservatory Class of 2009

My story begins four years ago, when I lived in the small and quiet community of Lake Arrowhead, California, which is located in the San Bernardino Mountains. My initial dance and vocal training began there. I always knew, however, that I wanted to pursue my dreams further and broaden my horizons as an artist. My first step to success was moving off the mountains and jumping forward to experience life in the real Orange County.

My entire family turned their lives around for me and moved off the mountains. My mother had heard from sources that the Orange County High School of the Arts was a highly respected and commended academic school. It also had the reputation of being a great performing arts school that fed talent to the entertainment industry. Before I knew it, my mom and I were off in the car looking forward to my first real audition. The audition for Mr. Paul, director of the honorable Music and Theatre Conservatory, was rather nerve-racking. I completed it, however, and was proud that I did the best I could do under the circumstances. I was nothing short of ecstatic when I received the letter stating that the school had accepted my talents into its community.

At first, I was honestly intimidated by the school, being only an innocent little seventh grader. Classes were held in an office-like tower. Although the high school students were much older, I quickly learned how generous, happy, and inspiring they all are. Now I look back and realize that coming to OCHSA may have been the best decision I have made thus far. It was genuinely life-changing. There is always something to learn from every single person here. I am so lucky in that my own mother was 200% supportive of my desire to attend.

No other high school, anywhere in the world, is remotely like OCHSA. Its many benefits make it stand out from the rest: Its environment is artistic and bohemian, the students want to go to school because they have auditioned and worked hard to get in, and everyone is supportive of each other's creativity, whether that creativity is expressed in an individual's art or even their personal style of clothing.

After having been here for three years, I remain grateful for the ongoing learning experience and artistic environment in which I find myself immersed. I have always been, and still am, proud to say that I go to the Orange County High School of the Arts. I contribute my soul and my style. It is more than worthwhile for any driven, artistic teenager to experience such a creative, rewarding, and supportive lifestyle.

OCHSA's Big 20

Brett Haynes
Instrumental Music Conservatory Class of 2009

All three years here have been great

A trashed out school in Santa Ana is what it ain't

It's this year that it's the big twenty

We've made our name and got it out there already

It's not just a school but a second home to some

If you haven't checked it out yet you should come

Every conservatory is unique and always amazing

The people around us are always commenting

Some say everything they see isn't far from Broadway

It's almost perfect and spectacular is what they say

I wish OCHSA many more years to come

It's sad to think I have only two years then it's all said and done

An Encouraging Environment

By Chantelle Gibbs
Music and Theatre Conservatory Class of 2009

A typical reaction I get when I tell people that I attend OCHSA goes a little something like this: "What do you study?", "Oh, I'm not talented enough to go there…", "Well that explains it." Or, the ever popular, "Oh….what is that exactly?" People eventually will dare to ask me what I will study in college. To be frank, I never have an answer. I still don't have an answer.

It's different being at an art school. You stay until 5:00 p.m. everyday. Your friends live 30 minutes away from you. You can get tests on chemistry and music theory on the same day. You can eat anywhere from the balcony of the second floor to the closed off Tenth Street down below. Your teacher graduated from the school you're attending. You pass by someone in a black trench coast and a tutu and don't even blink. It's hard to explain to other people.

OCHSA is where I am slowly realizing, day by day, what I will study. It may or may not be music and theater, which I absolutely love right now. Being involved in the arts is definitely something I dearly love and will always cherish. Every day, everything that I learn is something that I can take to any field in which I choose to work. The people that I meet, the advice I'm given, the choices I make, the differences I encounter, the challenges I face—everything and everyone has become a part of me.

It's always been especially difficult for me to realize my dream and actually strive to make it come true. It's a little discouraging now and then because my family can't always support the big aspirations I have because we are a single parent household. When my mom brought up the option of attending OCHSA, I immediately thought it would be too much for us

to handle. Yet the school is extremely understanding and compassionate. They will not turn down one who has potential but who is struggling because of certain hardships. It just proves that there is no one and nothing that could ever stop you from doing whatever you want to do.

It all starts with a dream. The power to make that dream come true is all up to you. Many choose to nurture their dream and attend OCHSA. It's there that we all learn about what it takes, how we'll do it, what might stop us, and where it can take us. You are learning right alongside people with the same hopes and aspirations as you. Although sometimes it can be hard to balance all the troubles and pressures, it truly is all worth it in the end. Every time I stay up late, every time I stress, every time I'm filled with doubt, I learn I must push myself to reach the goal.

I want to pursue a career in the musical theater department. However, I know deep inside how much effort it takes to be successful. It is not an easy thing. Still, I know that I have something kids at other schools don't have. I have teachers rooting for me the entire way. I have friends wanting to succeed as much as I. I have family supporting me 110%. It's the most encouraging environment one could ever be a part of.

So, whether you're sure of what you want to pursue or you still have no idea, whether you are a professional or an amateur, whether you are sure of your dream or you have yet to decide, the Orange County High School of the Arts is the place to be. It's the place to hope, the place to learn, the place to grow, the place to shine, for we are the stars of tomorrow.

The Best Years of My Life

By Kathryn Ruiz
Creative Writing Conservatory Class of 2007

In 2003 I was a freshman at a traditional public high school, left breathless at the enormity of the campus, the large student body, and almost impossible to navigate halls. I had pictured high school like I saw it depicted on television: funny teachers, clubs, and lifelong friendships rolled into four years amounting to "the best years of one's life." I tried to take advantage and got involved by joining marching band, the newspaper, and the literary magazine. I even made new friends. Things were going well.

But by the end of the first semester, I had witnessed numerous fights and had encountered drugs at school. Classes were all right, but no one was motivated and no one participated. I knew I didn't want to complete my education there. At the same time, a talent revealed itself. I began to write constantly—poetry in the margin of Spanish notes, novels during geometry class, and editing when I was home.

My mother heard of a rare high school for art students that boasted a Creative Writing Conservatory. I made an appointment for a tour and dropped off my application and portfolio. I still remember peering into a ceramics class and seeing all the students turn around to wave. Even at first glance, I could see the difference.

The next year I began high school again, but this time the school exceeded my expectations. OCHSA catered to the arts, but didn't slack when it came to academics. At OCHSA, I found motivation from staff, friendly competition with students, and some of the most interesting in-class discussions. I've loved every second of school spent with friends and teachers, and as graduation approaches, I'm sad to be leaving.

A Blessing

An Interview with Lauren Call

Music and Theatre Conservatory Class of 2007

Lauren: I'm Lauren Call, class president. I'm a representative for the school's student body and act as a liaison between students and the parents and school administration. I work with the student congress, which is a unique group that OCHSA has. The student congress provides a way for OCHSA's student body to communicate with the leadership class so that every student has a voice. I oversee the student congress, organizing the meetings and taking input from students, and then feeding that input into leadership class.

Interviewer: *Give me an example of an idea that a student has submitted that you made happen for them.*

Lauren: Right now we're working on senior privileges, which is something that we don't really have because we're such a new school. We're going to start senior activity days on Saturdays and Friday nights. We're also working on a pep rally, even though we don't have a football team.

Interviewer: *Why senior privileges?*

Lauren: We have a lot of privileges for everyone, but most schools have senior privileges. We want something for all the students to look forward to by the end of their term at OCHSA. We received input from all of the grade levels. They liked the idea because part of being a senior is being able to have a little something special before graduating high school.

Interviewer: *How long have you been at OCHSA?*

Lauren: I've been at OCHSA since seventh grade. I went to junior high at another school for three months. It wasn't a good environment for me. I heard that OCHSA was taking people later in the year, so I auditioned. I got in and I've just loved it ever since.

Interviewer: *How was the environment at your former school different from that at OCHSA?*

Lauren: In the middle school I went to the teachers were not supportive and

A Blessing

it wasn't a safe environment. Kids would make fun of each other. When I came here everyone was so accepting. It was such a community. Even though we have our differences, we all have respect for one another because everyone here is talented, and we all know that. Everyone here is special, so it's not an environment where kids make fun of or bully each other. There aren't as many cliques here. Everyone is friendly. The teachers here are much more supportive and much stronger academically. I came here and my test scores increased and my grades went up. It's just such a healthy environment. It's my home away from home.

Interviewer: *So take us on a day of the life of a student.*

Lauren: My classes all seem to be up on the higher floors of the school's seven-story tower building. So, I hike up to the sixth floor to get to class. It takes about five minutes to get my breath back and get situated. Then I go to class and basically participate in the academic classes that everyone else does at normal schools. Then, I have nutrition and go to another class. Then comes lunch. Lunch is really fun because you can go and visit with people around the school. On Fridays we play music, and everyone gets up and dances. Then I go to another academic class and then have conservatory. In conservatory, I learn about yourself and how to act. It's an outlet from all of the stress that I have during the day. And then I go home and do homework.

Interviewer: *Are you hoping to go into the arts afterwards?*

Lauren: I'm probably not going to go into my artistic field, but I know that what I learned in my conservatory has helped develop my confidence. It has also helped me with my leadership skills and my interpersonal skills. I've had so many different experiences with the people at OCHSA. Altogether, I feel I'm much more prepared to go to college.

Interviewer: *What kinds of activities or situations in the conservatory would prepare you for the workplace?*

Lauren: You learn how to speak and relate with people because in acting you have to work off of your partner during the entire perfor-

A Blessing

mance. You have to learn how to listen and cooperate and be part of a team because you are working with that person. You have to know that you can trust them and they can trust you. The same goes with working in any situation: you learn how to be a part of team and to be someone that people can trust and work with and admire.

Interviewer: *You mentioned that everyone is talented. Is there an element that you have to carry your own weight?*

Lauren: The competitive spirit at OCHSA is definitely a driving force for why people are successful at the school. It's not a bad competitive spirit; it's a good competitive spirit. It's a healthy sort of a competition as opposed to becoming jealous. It makes you want to do better. You don't want to let your teammates down, especially when you're doing scenes and monologues. And you can learn from your successes and the successes of other people. You can also learn from mistakes. For instance, when we practice monologues the teacher gives us notes on our performances and then we perform them again. In this way we're able to learn from our own experiences as well as what other people do and the mistakes they make.

Interviewer: *Is there anything that you would like us to know about OCHSA that you haven't said already?*

Lauren: I'd like to talk about the sense of community we have here. I feel like I'm part of a family when I come here, even though there's so many people that I don't know. You can go up to someone and smile at them in the hall, and they'll smile back. Everyone here really wants to be here. They're always nice and supportive. At other high schools not everyone can find their niche. It's sometimes difficult for them to feel like they're a part of a community. At OCHSA you feel like you belong from day one.

The minute I came to OCHSA I knew that this was where I was supposed to be. I've grown so much more as a person: I'm more confident, I'm more organized, I'm better at planning. It has been such a blessing in my life, because I know I wouldn't be the same person if I didn't go to school at OCHSA.

Odyssey in the Making

By Sara Blanton
Opera Conservatory Class of 2012

Orange County's Best
Rigorous
Ambitious
Numerous conservatories
Girls and boys come from near and far
Enlightening

Comprehensive education
Obviously the place everyone wants to be
Unity among the students
Notoriety for all
Talent
Youth at its best

Honorable quest
Invigorating atmosphere
Gifted
High achievers

Schools of instrumental music, classical and contemporary dance, and ballet folklorico
Conservatories of creative writing and instrumental music
Home to integrated arts, visual arts, and commercial dance
Opera, production and design, film and television, and music and theatre
Obtaining goals and dreams
Love of the arts

Odyssey in the making
Fun

Twenty years of success
Habits developed for a lifetime
ENCORE!

Academic honesty
Rewarding
Thrilled to be at the best school
Striving to be the best!!!

Not Afraid to Stand Up

An Interview with Ron Alatorre

Principal, Orange County High School of the Arts

Ron Alatorre currently serves as principal of the Orange County High School of the Arts. He studied music in college before entering the education profession. Alatorre taught in multiple disciplines, including English and music, before becoming an administrator. He holds a doctoral degree in education from the University of Southern California; a master's degree in educational administration from California State University, Fullerton; a professional administrative credential from California State University, San Jose; and a bachelor's degree in music from University of California, Los Angeles.

W alking around the classrooms, I watch different students as they're making presentations. When you see a classroom presentation at traditional schools, the students are typically bashful and awkward. They have not had many experiences performing. Communication is a major concept within the educational system, but many students are afraid to stand up in front of a class and communicate. They don't know how to present themselves, how to make a speech. At OCHSA, we have students more than willing to go up and make a presentation.

Communication is tremendous in the business world. People who are able to successfully deliver presentations will move further ahead than their peers who are afraid to stand in front of audiences. When I saw the ribbon cutting ceremony for the Ingram Micro Media Resource Center, we had students making wonderful presentations with the ease of true professionals. As high school students they already had the skills wrapped up. You rarely see college students able to do that.

I have traveled to Korea and studied their education program there. I have traveled to Japan and studied their programs there. People always compare the United States to what is going on there. The focus that we are able to offer at OCHSA is similar to the programs that I see overseas. At OCHSA, we leverage the motivation and skills of our students and staff and synthesize learning in both arts and academics. When our students take standardized tests, their high scores are a direct result of that synthesis. That's what differentiates us from other schools.

Looking at the vision of the school expanding along with the facilities is exciting. With that growth come a lot of challenges. There are the mundane things like managing the logistics of the student body as well as avoiding disruptions during construction. In addition, we have the more formidable challenge of achieving continuous improvement in our conservatories and academics. When you have a world-class institution, incremental improvement can become difficult, but we have managed to do it for years and we will continue to do so in the future. The proof will be through our performance in standardized test scores, which is especially important to the public, but also through ensuring that our students continue to grow and thrive as individuals and as a community of learners.

Every adult I've spoken to here has mentioned that they are here because of the students. The energy here is different and is exciting—it keeps us going. When I go home everyday I am able to say, "I've accomplished something. We're working hard at our vision and we've seen improvement." At night I find myself tired, but it's a good tired.

Making an Island an Oasis

An Interview with Chris Russell
Director, Instrumental Music Conservatory

Interviewer: *What brought you to OCHSA?*

Chris: I was brought to OCHSA by the Pacific Symphony. I had just finished doing the audition for the assistant conductor job there. Ralph was in communication with some of the administrators and they suggested he give me a try.

Interviewer: *So now do you teach somewhere else too?*

Chris: Right now I'm teaching at Cal State Fullerton. I teach theory classes there two mornings a week. I earned my bachelor's degree from Cal State Fullerton, so it's fun to be back there in another capacity.

Interviewer: *How do you feel OCHSA prepares students for college?*

Chris: I've had students come back to me and report on what they're doing in college. They always seem to say, "But I already did that at OCHSA." So that's an indicator to me that the training we're giving them not only prepares them for college, but gives them a level of repertoire, a level of education that in some cases is equal to what they might get in college.

Interviewer: *Now I know that you're really passionate about classical music. How do you feel that classical music prepares them to go into other fields?*

Chris: Well, for instance, being in an orchestra teaches students many different skills. They have to learn to play with someone else, to be a member of a team. If you're a violinist and you're playing something totally different than your stand partner, that's a problem—you're not being a member of the team. Yet, at the same time if you're a wind player, you are responsible for not only learning your individual assignment, but you are also responsible for enhancing the whole. In a sense, playing in an orchestra is analogous to any field you may work in that interfaces with others. People rarely work alone these days.

Making an Island an Oasis

Interviewer: *What do you get from the experience of standing in front of an orchestra on a typical Tuesday or Thursday afternoon?*

Chris: I get energy, motivation. The students have a desire to learn, a desire to be challenged which inspires the same in me. For me, that's extremely rewarding. Whenever I put a standard piece of music in front of a lot of these students, it's music they have never played it before. There's an air of discovery in rehearsal, an air that prompts them to say, "Yes, I'm in the presence of a great work of art." That's exciting, that's rewarding.

Interviewer: *You do some new music as well.*

Chris: Yes, I feel doing new music is important for the students because it gives them the breadth of what's out there. I don't want them to think the music stopped in 1900, because it didn't.

When I approach a new piece I don't approach it much differently than I do any other piece. I don't want them to feel that the music is weird. I also don't want to impose artificial restrictions. I want them to have an open mind. I usually give what I call "the new music speech." I tell them, "This may be something very different than what you've done before. I don't want you to judge the piece until after we have performed it. If you don't like it, that's fine. You don't have to like, for instance, any Beethoven symphony we play as long as you give it a chance and try to understand what it is the composer is saying."

I also try to bring in a lot of living composers as well, because we can't ask Beethoven what he meant by a certain passage. But you can ask a living composer like Brett Dean, who was here on campus in October. We were playing one of his pieces—a kind of quiet atmospheric piece. He came in and told us exactly what he had in mind when he composed it.

It was a powerful experience for the students to have the composer of the music they are learning standing in front of them explaining what he had in mind. It gives students a new perspective, because

Making an Island an Oasis

they begin to see that as performers we are actually re-creators. A composer creates something from nothing. We, as performers, re-create what the composer put on the page.

Interviewer: *Have you ever had a chance to perform a student composition?*

Chris: Sometimes. In fact, we're doing a piece now by one of our alum, Nicholas Urie. He wrote a jazz piece for orchestra and wanted to try it out because it's being premiered at the New England Conservatory next year. We also have a gifted composer in the orchestra who has won several awards already. We rehearsed and recorded one of his orchestra pieces so he could send it off with his college auditions.

Interviewer: *Can you tell us about Nicholas Urie?*

Chris: Sure. Nicholas Urie came to the school the first year OCHSA was in Santa Ana. That would be 2000. I recall he was eager to learn. I dare say he wasn't the most experienced player, but he had a lot of drive and motivation. Each year he was here he developed more and more and discovered his passions more and more by playing in the orchestra and playing some of the new pieces that we did.

I remember he had to do one crazy piece where he actually smashed bottles with a hammer. That's gone down in school lore as being one of the more infamous pieces that we've actually done. A lot of people from those years specifically remember us playing that composition.

I also remember his willingness to absorb new things. I teach a class here called Symphonic Literature, which is an overview of orchestral music. Each year I give the students a composer project. I typically assign a composer to a student that I think he or she might enjoy learning about. I gave Nicholas a maverick American composer named Charles Ives. I told him to write about his life and specifically on his composition "Three Places in New England."

His oral presentation still stands out in my mind as one of the best oral presentations I've ever heard. He said, "This is what I've really learned about the piece." He sat down at the piano and said, "This

Making an Island an Oasis

is what I really admire about his music." He then played some examples. It was a very personal presentation. I could tell studying and discovering his music made a big impact on him.

And now to see him at New England as a successful composer, playing vibes, straddling jazz and classical, and to see the successes that he's had is just incredible.

Interviewer: *I guess what I'd like to hear is why do you think it's important to have OCHSA here?*

Chris: A lot of students who come here were islands in their former schools. No one really understood them. No one really knew who Brahms is or cares who Brahms is. No one really understands if they say, "I really have to practice tonight." So when they come here, they're in an environment with people who think like them, who understand what it is that drives them and what their sense of art is all about. And you're with 1,300 students who understand that. So for a lot of these students they move from this island to an oasis.

Interviewer: *Will they find an oasis when they go out into the world or will OCHSA be a singular experience?*

Chris: I would hope students who go into the arts world, a college, university, or conservatory, find like-minded students. But I dare say that OCHSA is definitely a unique place. It's not often that you can take math classes with dancers and creative writers and painters and violinists all sitting together. That's unusual.

Interviewer: *And do the kids understand each other in their art form? Do they revere each other? What is the feeling students have toward each other?*

Chris: There is respect between what each of the different students do and how they perform. Just coming to concerts you can see different students from different areas watching their friends do what it is that they're here to do. It's also interesting having other faculty members, like the academic faculty, who might see a student sit at a desk all day have the opportunity to watch them perform onstage.

Making an Island an Oasis

Then finally it clicks, yes, this is why this student is here. They're here because they're an exceptional flute player, they're an exceptional trumpet player, they're an exceptional dancer.

Interviewer: *Does it work the other way around? Do you as one of the conservatory teachers ever marvel at the academic abilities of your students?*

Chris: Oh, absolutely. And I know sometimes I've had to ask students how to figure out a certain percentage or a math problem and they answer it like I was asking them to name the notes on a C major scale. I admire a lot of students for their academic prowess. I get that sometimes from some of the academic teachers who point out students who are great at science, or fantastic in math or who scored a perfect score on the math SAT. That sort of thing amazes me because I was never that type of student. I may have some talent, but it's not across the board like that.

The other thing you have to marvel at is that they get up at outrageously early hours. They find all these weird ways to get here—by bus, by train, by carpool—they get here and then they attend academic and conservatory classes until 5:00 p.m. Then they find their way home, arriving at 6:00 or 7:00 p.m. They might eat some dinner and then they do all their homework and practice until late and then they do it all over again. They still have a 4.3 GPA! I just don't get it, but then I really admire the students who do that, who can do that—and, trust me, there are a lot of students here who are able to do that.

Interviewer: *How many programs are you responsible for?*

Chris: The Instrumental Music Conservatory is comprised of different areas: the Jazz and Commercial Music Program, the Fennell Wind Studies Program, the Pianist Program, the Classical Guitar Program and the Orchestra Program.

Interviewer: *Five different groups. I assume when you came to this school 14 years ago you didn't plan to be running five groups within this school. What has that meant for you? Have you grown while you've been here?*

Making an Island an Oasis

Chris: When I started, the program was skeletal. Ralph gave me carte blanche to design and build the program. It has been a neat project to take it upon myself to make a difference. Then I watched it grow to a height that I would never have imagined 14 years ago.

I started the Symphony Orchestra ten years ago. It's actually the 11th year this year. If you would have told me then years ago that we'd be playing Beethoven's Ninth Symphony or that we'd be going to Carnegie Hall and performing with a 300-voice choir, I would have laughed. I would have said there's no way that that could happen, but it has happened.

So as the program has grown, there has obviously been more and more responsibility, but it helps that I can bring in these experts who know their craft so well and give the students valuable opportunities.

Running the Instrumental Music Conservatory at OCHSA has been rewarding. The privilege to work with all these experts and elevate the students to such high levels has been unique and wonderful.

Artwork by Alec Daigle, Visual Arts student

MUSIC

Photo by Molly Esposito, Visual Arts student

The OCHSA Experience

By Ameila Chen
Opera Conservatory Class of 2012

Now let me tell you a story, a tale
It's not like any other
It ranks a ten on the big grand scale
Unlike my fiddly brother

It starts with a lovely princess
Who's as stubborn as a reluctant mule
She hated change; she thought it grotesque
Yet somehow she kept her cool

Our princess has a mother
Who always wants the best
She found a school called OCHSA
And I'm sure you can figure out the rest

She waited until the school year ended
To tell her daughter this news
"Guess what!" she said "I found this school!"
The daughter knew this was the beginning of a battle, and
She knew she was going to lose

"This school I found, it's one of the best!
It's ranked one of the top in the state!"
"I don't care how great it is. I'm not moving now!"
Said the daughter, but she then knew her fate

"The greatest part is that you must audition,
For this is an arts school."
Said the mother, "It's easy; you'll do ballet."
But the daughter shouted, "I don't want to dance all day!"

At first the answer was "no"
Because all the spots were full
Then when a spot opened up
The mother had to push and pull

The princess auditioned late;
It was the second to last day of registration
She dances with commercial dancers
But the whole while she was filled with frustration

Although she loved the place and the teachers
The expressions on her face were all ugly features
The mother still knew she would be the winner
And she offered to take them both out to dinner

The plan did not work
For it was still lunch time
They went out to a museum instead
To a restaurant, fancy and fine

Fifteen minutes into the lunch
The mother got a call
The call upset the princess very much
And the mother saw her face fall

She had gotten into the school
She would have to try it now
She thought she would act like a fool
Yet she managed to suppress a small, "Wow!"

Her mother went to register for her
Got all her textbooks and such
School started in two days, "Yikes!" she thought
She hated to be in a rush

When she started the first day
She realized what a great day it was
She didn't know why she had made such a fuss
She knew that this school was a must

Finally she opened her eyes
She heard what a teacher had to say
"The OCHSA experience is what you make of it."
And she knew she was there to stay

On Every Corner a Starbucks;
In Every City an OCHSA

An Interview with Samantha Mo
Faculty Member, Orange County High School of the Arts

Samantha: My name is Samantha Mo and I teach seventh and eighth grade English at OCHSA. This is my fourth year teaching at OCHSA and I love it. My coming here was truly serendipitous. Originally, I was offered a job from Anaheim School District, but was waiting for an offer from OCHSA. I was about to sign my paperwork with Anaheim when the OCSHA offer came in. It was perfect timing.

I grew up excelling in academics, but at the same time having a passion for dance and choreography. So I understand and relate to the kids here—they want to excel academically and they also have an artistic passion. Being able to work in a school that fosters vigorous academics as well as an artistic passion is a dream come true for me.

Interviewer: *How did you hear about OCHSA?*

Samantha: Somebody had told me about OCHSA. I had never heard of programs or a school such as OCHSA. Right away I imagined OCHSA like that 80's television show *Fame*. I pictured kids dancing, and there'd always be tubas or guitars or something being tuned in the background. I found out about an opportunity online and applied. In my first year, I learned that OCHSA was actually one of the top five high schools in Orange County. That was amazing to me. To know that it had a reputation for being an original charter school to have a focus in the arts, as well as academics, was already enough of an incentive for me to come and work here. Then to know that it was supported by excellent teachers and high academics, that was an additional plus.

Interviewer: *Where were you before OCHSA?*

Samantha: I had just completed my teaching credential and master's over at UCI. I was student teaching at a junior high in Garden Grove. It was vastly different from OCHSA. The students were wonderful, but there's something special about OCHSA students. Even coming in as seventh and eighth graders they are already self-motivated, they're aware of their

On Every Corner a Starbucks;
In Every City an OCHSA

passions, they have big dreams, and are filled with such confidence and enthusiasm, an energy that is unparallel to any other school I've visited or taught at.

There is also energy amongst the teachers. They are allowed a lot of creative latitude to reach these kids and to bring out their best, whether it is in their academic disciplines or conservatories. To teach and work in this environment is liberating and fun.

Interviewer: *Do you have favorite stories about the kids?*

Samantha: One situation with one student in my second year of teaching was momentous to me. It woke me up and allowed me to understand why this is such a special place and why it's great to work here. The student was an eighth grader who demanded just a little bit more attention. He had weak organizational skills and, like a typical eighth-grade boy, was a bit distracted and had a hard time doing his homework. So I needed to support him and give him a little bit more guidance. At the end of the year, I witnessed him dance in *Broadway Bound*. I was floored by his tap dancing, his presence, his confidence, and his joy. In retrospect I realized that he reminded me, as a teacher, that my role is to give these kids everything I can to help them excel. It taught me to use my imagination to see the amazing possibilities that these kids can achieve. My role as a teacher is to provide them with as many opportunities as I can for them to develop the extraordinary skills and talents that they have inside of them, skills and talents that need encouragement and the right conditions to blossom.

In a typical classroom, you don't see these kids come out this way. In a typical classroom you look at their organizational skills, their reading, their writing.

That is the wonderful thing about OCHSA; it gives these kids an opportunity to explore different gifts and to explore creativity in different ways. To be able to write lesson plans and come up with reading and writing activities that will bring out that same enthusiasm. It's exciting.

85

On Every Corner a Starbucks; In Every City an OCHSA

Seeing this boy dance and the way he came across made me want to rewrite my curriculum so that I could better support kids like that.

Interviewer: *It sounds like that is the aspect of your job which gives back to you. That is, the kids are giving back to you.*

Samantha: Definitely. They give me hope, they remind me to dream big. They give me so much energy. They're eclectic, they know who they are, and they experience a freedom and confidence that I'd like every kid to experience.

Interviewer: *So where would you like to see OCHSA go?*

Samantha: I would like to see OCHSA in the pocket of every neighborhood, because I think it provides something that I think every kid would just love to experience. So beyond just having a theater here, beyond just having more students, I would like to see OCHSA franchise and become like Starbucks and be in every city.

Interviewer: *If you had a big donor sitting right in front of you who could really help the school in some way, what would say to them to get them on board?*

Samantha: I believe every person has been endowed with creativity. In our current public education system there's not a focus on the arts. The wonderful thing about OCHSA is it allows students to tap into creativity in problem solving, in learning, in decision making, and in artistic form. Whether or not they continue to pursue these artistic endeavors, they are part of an academic learning environment which fosters learning as well as creativity. I am hoping that with your generosity you might sponsor OCHSA to allow students who may not have that opportunity in a regular public school to experience the unique opportunity to develop and realize their creative potential in academics as well as arts. Who knows, you might be sponsoring the next Martha Graham, Albert Einstein, or Bill Gates.

Painting by Emily Smith, Visual Arts alumna

And the Story Goes On

An Interview with the Sparks Family

Jaime Sparks is a first year alumna of the Orange County High School of the Arts and currently serves as President of the school's Alumni Association. Her daughter, Paige, is currently a student in OCHSA's Pianist Program. Her youngest child, Sydney, is an aspiring stage actress.

Jaime: It all happened my senior year. I remember it being such a hard thing. I seriously was torn because on one hand I wanted to spend my senior year with the kids I grew up with, but on the other hand the arts in my school were not looked upon with the same esteem as they were at OCHSA. Frankly, everybody looked down upon the arts. I kicked and screamed that I didn't want to go, but my mom said I had to.

My first day at OCHSA was the most amazing experience. There was an energy; a spirit that I immediately felt the second I stepped onto the campus. To have that kind of spirit, to be in the company of other students who felt the same way about the arts and who had similar aspirations was incredibly motivating and exciting. When I walked into zero period choir of all things, the entire football team was sitting there amongst everybody. It was a huge class, probably a hundred kids, and they were just singing away. That was my first experience inside of OCHSA.

I did a lot of film and television, commercials, and voiceovers. I've traveled all over the world with The Young Americans. I've sung with Opéra Pacific and LA Opera. To this day, I can just go into a voiceover and sing an area, maybe rehearse a few times prior to that, put it down on track and there it is. I'm still doing that.

I am excited to put both Paige and Sydney into piano because I want them to have that edge when they're older. I want them to be able to pick up a piece of music and be able to read it and play it. Developing those types of skills today will help them to succeed in whatever they do tomorrow.

And the Story Goes On

Paige: I decided to go to OCHSA in fifth grade because of my mom. I auditioned for Integrated Arts, for seventh grade, last year and it wasn't that difficult. I did three things: my visual, my singing, and my piano. They didn't expect that. Ms. Stafford thought I was only going to do my visual and my singing. She was surprised when I said I was going to play piano as well.

A friend of mine had auditioned around the same time, and she was accepted before I was. I was getting nervous. Then I received my acceptance letter. I was so excited. Well, in my first year we did a lot of things—visual, voice, and film and television, which I really liked. Exploring different arts directed me to my musical path.

I have been playing the piano for about nine years now. I believe it's my calling. Everybody I know in that conservatory is amazing; they all play concertos and sonatas. They inspire me to get better and better.

I would like my sister, Sydney, to come to OCHSA, too. She's a really good student; she gets her work done. She has a high grade point average. I know she would do great here.

Sydney: I don't know. I think it's really nice that Paige thinks that I am going to make it to OCHSA. I really do want to make it into OCHSA. I hope she's right. If I don't make it, I'll probably be miserable for the rest of my life.

Jaime: Drama Queen.

All: (laughter)

Photo by Molly Esposito, Visual Arts student

Art in the Community

An Interview with Patricia McMaster
Director of Community Programs

Pat McMaster has been involved with OCHSA since 1995 when her son was accepted into the music and theatre program at Los Alamitos High School. She currently serves as the school's Director of Community Programs, overseeing the Foundation's Camp OCHSA and California ARTS Center programs.

We came to see a play at OCHSA, since one of my son's friends was in the play. He said, "This is the place where I want to be. This is where I want to go." So, he auditioned and he got accepted. It was one of the most memorable moments for us as parents. All four years that he spent at OCHSA were an amazing opportunity for him to grow as a person and as an artist. We saw early on the difference that OCHSA made in our son's life, so we decided to become parent volunteers.

For the four years that my son was a student at the school, my husband and I were involved as parent volunteers for the Music and Theatre productions. Later on, I became a member of the school's Foundation Board of Directors. My son graduated in June of 1999. Two weeks later, I came to work at OCHSA. I left my old company after 24 years to work at OCHSA because I believed in the program; I believed in the vision. I saw the impact that the experience of going to OCHSA had on my son, the motivation it gave him to pursue his dreams and to be a better person. Later, he actually taught at the school for two years as an elective teacher. So it was just an amazing experience for my husband and me as parents, and it continues to be a rewarding and amazing experience for me now as a staff member.

I currently handle the school's community outreach programs. When I started to work at OCHSA, I was the public relations and marketing person. When we moved from Los Alamitos to Santa Ana, one of the goals that Ralph had was to give something back to the community in Santa Ana. Part of our charter was to bring some awareness of the school to the Santa Ana community. We started Camp OCHSA five years ago, and since then we have served more than 2,000 students. We offer two sessions during the school year, a fall and a spring session, which bring in 350 kids from different areas in Santa Ana. We also train our own students to become counselors and to be the teachers for the younger kids. It energizes me everyday when I come to work and when I interact with the students, staff, parents, and community.

The Camp OCHSA program is conducted in both English and Spanish. The majority of the students, I would say 99%, speak Spanish. The classes we provide to them are in dance—ballet and jazz—singing, drama, and visual arts. The students select one area to focus on. We utilize OCHSA staff as coordinators and they oversee the student volunteers. The student volunteers earn service hours for the college applications. Altogether, it's a wonderful experience for our students as well as coordinators and student teachers. I am pleased to know that what I do at OCHSA makes a difference in the community where we work. Overseeing the California ARTS Center Program is also another positive experience because we are able to provide opportunities for other children to benefit from the art classes we offer on Saturdays, Monday nights, and the six-week summer program.

91

OCHSA Is Everything

By Sarah Waters
Integrated Arts Conservatory Class of 2012

It was my first year at OCHSA; I was so thrilled to begin

Because here being unique is another word for fitting in

I'm so excited to be a part of this amazing school

Because there are no guidelines to being popular or cool

The food is great, the teachers too

The stairs are still a bit annoying, but what are you going to do

I love OCHSA, more than I thought I ever would

There's nothing to complain about because everything is good

The school has everything; you'd be silly to disagree

When I'm here, I don't feel fake, I simply feel like me

Teaching from Experience

An Interview with Jim Kolb
Director, Commercial Dance Conservatory

I danced professionally for about 20 years. I've done concert dance, television work, film and videos, and musical stage productions. I've done a wide variety of work in dance, and I've been pretty successful at it. Dance was my first love, of course. When I came out to the West Coast I worked especially hard at my dancing technique. Working professionally as a dancer will do that to you. It takes effort to stay on top of your game. But I enjoyed it, even the night club work, going to Vegas, Reno, and Tahoe, you name it.

When I was ready to move on to teaching, I taught at Glendale College and Whitman College during the summers. I also did two years at USC as a dance instructor. Then I was asked to start teaching here. I have spent a wonderful 19 years teaching here.

Of course, opening this facility six years ago was a big undertaking. I was personally teaching from 7:30 in the morning, when they had their conservatory classes, and then we went directly into electives. So I was teaching the elective course, which is generally the PE dance courses, and then going right into my conservatory classes. As a director I've never had to teach that much, but we all pitched in. We did what we could do just to give the school a good start and get the students coming here and make it work. But it just about killed me that year. That beginning year was difficult but it was well worth it.

My whole philosophy in running the Commercial Dance Conservatory is to make these kids as marketable as possible so that they can have successful, consistent careers. The only way I know how to do that is to give them a wide range of dance—they have to do it all—and to teach them the skills that enabled me to be successful in my dance career. I didn't have to go do a waiter's job or something to make ends meet. If I wasn't dancing professionally, I was teaching.

We are also bringing in guest choreographers, guest artists to teach master classes and set choreography on our students. It's an incredible experience for the students. They are learning new and current dance styles. Artists who are out there working professionally come in and work with these students. In commercial dance we try especially hard to get the most contemporary work that's happening in the industry so that our students have first-hand direction and instruction on what it entails.

Teaching from Experience

Many colleges and universities tend to be about the faculty. I'm sure they have some guest choreographers to come in and work with them, but we try to get as much of a variety going here as we possibly can. The result is that our students get exposed to all different types of choreography so they can make an educated choice as to where they want to go with their career and with their passion that they foster here.

The students I'm most proud of are the ones who have gone into dance companies. We have a male student who just graduated last May and has now gone on to Alvin Ailey American Dance Theater in New York. We had a student two years ago who is now in Dance Theatre of Harlem. We have a graduate who is at Juilliard and another at Harvard. Did I ever think that Harvard would be a dance place? No. But she's making the best of it. Since Harvard is close to New York, she's making that transition and studying at Harvard. She did so well academically, and we're proud of her accomplishments. Those are the kind of things—whether it's academics or college or dance companies or even in the professional field—of which I stand in amazement.

My dream is to have music theory for dancers so that they can make the transition from reading a score to being able to count that score and being able to choreograph to it. It would be a remarkable thing for their future creativity, and many of them do want to go into the choreographing. Maybe they don't have the desire to dance professionally; maybe their gift is to choreograph. Many do have that gift, and we try to nurture it with a student choreography concert once a year. Our senior conservatory owns the whole show: They do the choreography, the costuming, the collaboration, with the production and design kids to do their own lighting. It's a fully student produced show. And I must say it's one of our most popular and successful shows that we run throughout the year.

We're building the cake in layers. The icing on the cake is going to come when we have a beautiful theater that we can call our own. To have hands-on ownership of that facility is going to be a remarkable icing on the cake. We are continuing to build, as I said, in layers. And the layers will just keep rising until we do get that icing. Then we will be complete.

A Poem: By Two Pleased OCHSA Parents

Anonymous
Instrumental Music Conservatory Class of 2003
Film and Television Conservatory Class of 2006

What will happen with your child here,
Be it son or be it daughter
They will become who they are
And will sparkle like soda water
In every way, they will see
What it's like to work hard
They will see what they are made of
And will build character and regard

They will see what it's like
To win or to lose
They will see what it's like
To have to choose
From better or best
It's never easy
Because the company they keep here
Will never make it breezy

The kids at OCHSA are unlike any other
And care about each other like sister and brother
They compete for the spots
In the dance or the play
But respect each other deeply
And would have it no other way

They rehearse and practice, but they have fun
Dance and sing and jump and run
No, no football, and no, not a mascot
Not a track and nary a basket

But they do have clubs like any school
And a leadership class that is elected to rule

Academic teachers teach English, history,
and French
They teach physics, math, and chemistry
They teach it from the bench
Side by side with the arts folks
They are working in every way
To make sure your artful child
Can go to college at the end of their stay

The arts teachers see your child
As a piece of molding clay
They shape them and they carve them
And try to make their day
They see themselves in your child
Many years ago,
And want to do their darndest
To help them learn and grow

This is a school, a community
A culture for the best
While here your child will blossom
And be put to the test
But when they're through and graduate
You'll know you've chosen well
This school is just plain awesome
And that's all there is to tell

Keeping the Dream Alive

An Interview with Russell R. Stern
OCHSA Parent and Foundation Board Member

I became involved with OCHSA after attending one of the school's Season Finale performances. After attending the finale, I just fell in love with the school. I think Ralph pretty much knew he had me hooked by that point. For both my wife and I, the arts are an important part of our family life. Patti was an art teacher for many years at the middle and high school levels; I'm a frustrated guitarist who tries to play and keep up with my son, who is now a student here at OCHSA this year. So, we love the arts and think it's important that they stay funded—and, of course, that's just not happening in public schools these days.

We've been involved because we love the arts. We love what the school does. We love the talent that it produces, the great students that come here, and the environment that they nurture. I've heard student stories, probably hundreds of them by now, and every student says the same thing: At no other place could they feel so much at home for what they are and what they do and what they're about than OCHSA.

The guy that always sticks out for me, and who probably keeps me here more than anyone, is Ralph. I think my energy and drive comes in part from his energy and his passion to just keep doing it 20 years in a row. It's inspiring to me. It's inspiring to be a participant in the school, but it's also inspiring in my own life to just watch his passion for what he's doing.

We've gone through several transitions in the Foundation: the transition from struggling financially to really building a support base for the school to carry out its mission. I think the next vision for the school is to build out the facilities at the performing arts center, build out and finish our facilities here and create a footprint for the school that will allow it to continue forever. Beyond that, I'd love to see OCHSA replicated across the country.

THE CONNECTIONS

*"No man is an island, entire of itself;
every man is a piece of
the continent, a part of the main."*

--MEDITATION XVII, JOHN DONNE

Landscape by Jennifer Lee, Visual Arts alumna

Batman and Butterflies

By Debbie Kristiansen
Orange County High School of the Arts Parent

My 15-year-old son, Geoffrey, is a die-hard superhero fan. While almost any superhero will do, his highest admiration is reserved for Spiderman and Batman who alternately take the lead. Action figures, comic books, posters, and movies claim the top of his Christmas and birthday wish lists (until he recently discovered cash). His character t-shirts were the mainstay of his wardrobe since his toddler days. In preschool, if his Batman shirt with the attached cape was dirty, he'd make do with a baby towel snug on his head, the white cotton cape flying behind him, just like Batman's as he swoops into the Batmobile or Superman as he flies above the skies of Metropolis. Mom's old scarves also made great capes.

Unfortunately, around fourth grade, the boys at school starting teasing Geoffrey about his Spiderman shirts and his Batman lunchbox, so we begrudgingly packed them up. For a quiet kid who struggled to fit in socially, there seemed no other practical option. We bought far fewer character shirts in the coming years, and he wore them only with accepting family and friends.

But then OCHSA came into our lives, a change that brought excitement, uncertainty, and hope. In August of this year, with a huge smile on my face and a knot in my throat, I watched as my high school freshman left home for his first day at OCHSA—wearing a black shirt with the bold Batman logo. My boy was back.

When he called me at my office that afternoon, I was full of the usual questions: "How was your first day?", "Do you like your teachers?", "Who did you eat lunch with?", "Did carpool work out OK?" In the middle of answering he offered, "Hey Mom, I think it's fine to wear my character shirts to OCHSA, because there was a kid there today wearing butterfly wings." And so it turns out that my son is actually rather mainstream in this wonderful place of tolerance and originality. Even if he never works in his chosen artistic option, his life will be improved dramatically by being accepted and learning to be more so himself.

The Freedom to Be Me

By Alyssa Haynie
Visual Arts Conservatory Class of 2007

The day I met one of my first friends at the Orange County High School of the Arts he was dressed as Alex de Large from *A Clockwork Orange*. Over the next few years, my assorted friends would dress as clowns, priests, and Hunter S. Thompson.

I had come from a fundamental middle school that looked like a boat and a prison at the same time. It wasn't a boat. Through some clever use of administrative whiteout, uniforms were made mandatory. This is illegal in public schools, but to mask any inconsistencies in policy, the term "fundamental" was splashed into the troughs of parents who didn't care enough to find out what it meant.

A neatly stapled packet of research (assembled by my tiny seventh grade hands) lay on the desk of Lucinda Clear, our principal, along with a cover letter explaining how I would make copies and distribute them if students weren't allowed uniform waivers if they wanted them. One extremely unproductive meeting later and I was at OCHSA just in time for its second quarter.

I was embraced by a group of rough and tumble, neon loving individuals. If I wore an ostentatious prom dress, no one cared. If I wore a telephone cord for a belt or headband, it wouldn't matter. I was dancing and I was loving and I was breathing. I was happy. An environment that nurtured my creativity let me make my own mistakes and my own progress. I could grow into who I was and not be reprimanded for it. It was that freedom that allowed me to grow into the person I am today.

Here Thar Be Dragons

By Alexandria Murillo
Creative Writing Class of 2008

Imagine a girl at the age of five. Give her light brown hair, blue eyes, and a slight short build. Put her in a navy jumper, and then place her in a kindergarten filled to the brim with other cookie cutter children the same age. At first she's enough the same as the rest of them: the right age and size—even imaginative and hyperactive. For a few years, everything is fine; all of them live in a world of magic and dragons.

Five years pass. The summer of fourth grade comes to a close, and the cookie cutter children return to school for fifth grade. So big, so mature, in the 'big kid' building now, with only three years of elementary school left. This is the big year—the year they learn about drugs, the year older brothers and sisters teach them vocabulary that's in no teacher's lesson plan. The children now look at life with their new little raisin eyes and are ready to leave behind the marshmallow igloos, entering what the adults have dubbed reality. Slowly, the magic fades into science and religion; the dragons turn into newts. They leave one by one, until eventually only three with chocolate chip eyes, the girl among

Photo by Mary Amor, Visual Arts alumna

Here Thar Be Dragons

them, is left behind to dance with dragons.

Sixth grade comes, another year lost. One of the chocolate chip children escapes, and then there are two. While the others melt together in little groups, secure in their definition for the duration of their stay, they dance from clump to clump, always on the outskirts, always the oddballs. Different, but at least different together, they cling to each other like sole survivors of a sunken vessel, finding venire solace in their twin outcast places.

Seventh grade. The other chocolate chip survivor is rescued by the call of another middle school. Two minus one leaves the brown-haired girl, now twelve, with only the depths of her imagination to keep her company. They call her weird, childish, the strange one. They warn in whispers that she might have rabies. They act to the scripted lines of stereotypical high school kids, the jocks and the preps and the Goths—tadpoles trying to act like sharks. She's somewhere else, sitting in the trees and the wind, finding reprieve in the pen and paper. She traps the memories of the world they used to play in there, living in the past to avoid the present she can't escape.

Eighth grade students, top dogs now. They've risen to the peak, and have nowhere to go but down. But the spiral still looks a long way off and now they want to enjoy the view. Chests puffed and croaking their own superiority, they've changed from tadpoles to bullfrogs. The girl is nothing now, neither cookie cutter nor amphibian, but a light spray of mist floating around and jotting down the webs in her mind onto paper. The oth-ers prepare to enter a bigger pond that they call high school, most going to Mater Dei. But she's found hope, not a pond, but a mystery. A place named OCHSA. Shrouded by mist, light emanates from the core, and in the core is where her escape, her writings, will save her, if she gets in. It's her one chance, and she risks it. Now the looks, the ostracizing, and condescending tones are nothing but the buzzing of the flies they eat. The wait, the suspense, consumes her. One chance, one hope, it all rests on the letter.

The letter comes, small and white, and she almost cries on the spot, certain of rejection. But, still clinging to hope, wishing on the hidden stars, she opens it. The magic words, CONGRATULATIONS YOU HAVE BEEN ACCEPTED! She does cry now, tears of joy. Eighth grade ends, goodbyes are said. Fake tears on their part; fake tears on hers. The façade can be kept up for one more day, for the teachers' and parents' sake. Summer comes, never less welcome, never so long.

Finally the summer clears, revealing the mountain up ahead. She arrives on the first day into its protective caverns. Inside, she finds others like herself, with chocolate chip eyes and the label of weird. The mundane life she'd been living fades back to magic, and the newts grow into dragons.

Being Seen

By Tony Wong
Orange County High School of the Arts Parent

It was Thursday, October 31, 2002—an OCHSA school day that was also Halloween. OCHSA encouraged the students to dress up. Our daughter Rebecca was in the eighth grade and she got dressed up in her costume. Even though she is a music and theatre student and quite comfortable on stage, she was self-conscious in public settings. So on her way to OCHSA, she was embarrassed to be seen in costume by the public. The entire way to OCHSA, she sat as low as possible in the car as my wife drove.

When my wife made the turn from Main Street onto Tenth Street and entered "OCHSA space," Rebecca proudly sat up. She didn't seem embarrassed anymore. Curious, my wife asked why she suddenly sat up so confidently. Rebecca replied that she didn't feel out of place now that they were close to school. OCHSA students and teachers were not judgmental.

"They're all doing strange things all the time so nobody is surprised. Besides, people at OCHSA are considered 'cool' if they're original and creative," Rebecca told my wife. Rebecca got out of the car in full regalia and walked to her class without hesitation.

I remember when I was in high school. I spent most of my school life, especially at the lower grade level, trying to stay "under the radar." I didn't want to stand out for fear of being ridiculed. Only the most popular kids could get away with being different or expressing themselves in creative, unique ways. My fellow regular high school students looked at those popular "special people" as trendsetters. Regular high school was a reflection of society with its constant peer pressure to remain "normal." It was an unspoken protocol to which students felt obligated to conform. What makes OCHSA so special for our kids is that *not conforming* is what they conform to.

Finding Mirandah

By Margie Smith
Visual Arts Conservatory Parent

It has been over four years ago since an acquaintance told me about OCHSA. Her daughter, Taylor, was thriving at the school. She encouraged me to have my own daughter, Mirandah, try out for seventh grade. That was probably the best advice I have ever received.

Mirandah had always done well in school both academically as well as socially, but sixth grade was different. The school she was at did not accept her. She was different, immature compared to her peers. Mirandah had always been a bubbly, energetic child who walked around singing and dancing; however, I began to notice her personality drastically change. Mirandah did not feel comfortable at her school. She was being bullied and ridiculed by kids because of her love for the arts.

It did not take a lot of encouragement to get Mirandah to agree to try out for OCHSA. She had attended Camp OCHSA ever since she was in fourth grade and loved the idea of going there for school.

Mirandah and I discussed what conservatory she would like to try out for. She immediately chose dance. Mirandah started dancing at age seven, which is when she decided she would become a dancer. We had been told to have her try out for at least two conservatories, so I suggested she try visual art. After waiting what seemed

to be forever, the letter finally came. We anxiously opened it. Much to Mirandah's disappointment, she didn't make into dance. But she did make it into visual art. She must have called everyone she knew. A feeling of relief came over me. Mirandah no longer would be the misfit at school; she would become one of many different misfits that make up OCHSA, a school where she could be herself.

As I look back at Mirandah's years at OCHSA, I see so many positives. The teachers I must commend. They go out of their way to help each child. A few years ago, Mirandah was diagnosed with a visual perception disability, one that requires special accommodations in class. Her teachers have all been supportive and encouraging. I can't imagine where Mirandah would be if it weren't for OCHSA. She has received a wonderful education and has found a love for art that may never have been uncovered without this opportunity. As of now Mirandah is planning a career in photography, all because of a teacher that believes in her.

The Actor

By Hannah Solow

Music and Theatre Conservatory Class of 2008

My friends party. Well, they aren't really my friends anymore. They used to be my friends. Let me start over. My ex-friends party. They don't like school. They are disruptive at the movies. They judge people based on the brand of handbag they are carrying. They think drinking Peach Smirnoff is cool. After we left elementary school and parted ways, I realized what truly different paths we had taken. The path I chose was past the alcohol and adolescent troubles and straight on to OCHSA. While I do not think if I had not gone to OCHSA I would have become a crack smoking delinquent, I do feel that OCHSA has shaped me into my best self. Having the focus and passion I have in musical theater has developed me into a person I know I would not be if I had gone to a different school.

I cannot judge what goes on at the high school I would have gone to, as I have never attended. However, my old friends do go to that school. They have stories that I cannot relate to. They are often confused by OCHSA, as are most people. You don't have a football team? There aren't any pep rallies? What do you mean you don't have a gym? The list of questions goes on and the answers are usually the same. No, we don't have a football team, pep rallies, or a gym. But we do have art shows, musicals, and movie showings. It's funny because these are the social events of OCHSA. When I ask my friends at the other high school what their musical is, they usu-

ally respond that they never even knew they did a musical. Or if they do know, it is not the hippest thing to go do on a Friday night.

As a gregarious person, I do not think I would lack friends at the other high school. I would probably hang out with my old friends, but I would also want to do theater. I would be stuck on the balance beam walking the thin line between drama geek and social butterfly. OCHSA lets me be both. Everyone is free to be who he or she wants to be. OCHSA provides a creative and safe environment in which students can grow and challenge themselves. I challenge myself every day, whether it is doing aikido rolls on the floor of the cafeteria or singing a new song in front of my music and theatre voice class.

As I continue to study drama and voice, I become more passionate about it. When I first began, I simply enjoyed it. It was a hobby. I sang in the car and was a ham in front of the class. I feel OCHSA, its teachers, and classes were able to turn my ordinary qualities into ones that can one day become extraordinary. I find myself constantly singing. I sing so incessantly that I am often yelled at to shut up. My relatives are always asking me about the shows I am doing. This is who I am, and everyone knows it. I have become the musical theater girl, the actor. It almost makes me feel important. I know what I am doing with my life. It gives me a sense of security.

The Actor

Last year I was fortunate enough to be cast in OCHSA's "Performing with the Pros." We performed on stage with the Tony-nominated actress Alice Ripley. It was an amazing experience I will never forget. It is cliché to say that, but if you have that sort of experience, it's hard to describe it any other way. We had rehearsals almost every day after school for two straight weeks. I would come home around nine o'clock, tired and wanting to crawl onto the floor and sleep. I would have hours of homework to do, but somehow it didn't matter. Those long nights were worth it the pleasure I got from every moment I spent with my cast. Sitting on the floor during rehearsal, listening to the beautiful music we were making, I felt completely content.

I think it is too harsh to say that musical theater saved my life. I have enough confidence in myself to say I would have succeeded in any field I put my mind to. But I do feel that without OCHSA I would be another person than who I am today. Who knows if that would be good or bad, but I like who I am now. Musical theater has given me happiness that I plan to follow the rest of my life. It has given me direction. While I have friends who don't know if they want to become a doctor in a world famous hospital or an acrobat in Cirque du Soleil, I know that musical theater is the career I want to pursue. When I am on *Conan O'Brien* or taking an interview with *People* magazine, I plan on thanking OCHSA for its endless lessons and support.

Sketch by Molly Esposito, Visual Arts student

A Discover of Color

By Jessica Cobarruvias
Visual Arts Conservatory Class of 2007

I come from a family of immigrants whose only hope for their children was that they obtain an education. There was never a thought of excelling in any subject other than academics, because art was a luxury and not a subject. It wasn't until fifth grade when I participated in a special art class that I discovered the wondrous world of art and absolutely fell in love with it. After my first class, I knew that I was serious about art. After that first day of art class, I researched artists and discovered their work. I could not attend art classes because my parents simply could not pay for them, so I took it upon myself to learn about art.

When I enrolled in intermediate school, I knew my parents could not afford outside art classes, so I didn't even ask. I decided I would take the art classes offered by my school as an elective. I was fascinated with everything I learned: the history, the artists, and the techniques. I was fortunate enough to have one of the best art teachers in my district. I was involved in a special studio art program after school where I gained further knowledge of art. In my art class, we went to museums, plays, and even had our own art show.

By the middle of eighth grade, my teacher informed me about OCHSA and the tremendous opportunities that were offered there. I had no idea that such a prestigious school was right in my city. I then realized that I could never make it into OCHSA because I had never attended an art class outside of school and would be auditioning with kids who had taken classes and had more experience than I. I decided to apply anyway and was given the application by my teacher. I filled it out and gave it to my mom to sign. That's when she found out I was applying. She was astonished that I had done this all by myself. She realized that I was serious about art. I was really depressed for a couple of weeks, but I applied and was determined to make my audition the best it could be. I attended an audition workshop with the Visual Arts Conservatory director. I was the only one who showed up and was given a one-on-one consultation. That meeting with the director gave me the confidence to believe in myself because she said that I had talent.

I finally went to the audition. I was overjoyed when I was accepted. I couldn't believe it. The first few days were tough because I did not know a soul and was not used to being the minority. I was uncomfortable with such a diverse student body. I then met some friends and realized there was nothing to be uncomfortable about—we were all there for the same reasons. I learned to accept who I was and started making friends from every single conservatory.

Not only is OCHSA a great art school, the

A Discover of Color

academics are superb. In addition, this is the first school that I have attended where teachers actually care about the students. There is so much motivation and positive energy at OCHSA that every single student wants to be a better person because they know people believe in them. I love everyone at OCHSA because we are all a support network.

I am now in my senior year. I can honestly say the past four years have been the best of my life. I have learned how to interact with other cultures, and I have made friendships that will last a lifetime. OCHSA is a community where everyone is accepted.

Without OCHSA I would have attended a traditional public high school and would not have pursued art seriously. OCHSA saved my life with art. It has enabled me to excel, opened cultural barriers, and introduced me to the real world. My family now understands the importance of art in my life because I use it to express who I am. The happiness it brings to my life is essential. I thank OCHSA for giving me the opportunity to experience art at the professional level that otherwise would not have been available. I will always have OCHSA in my heart.

Photo by Mary Amor, Visual Arts alumna

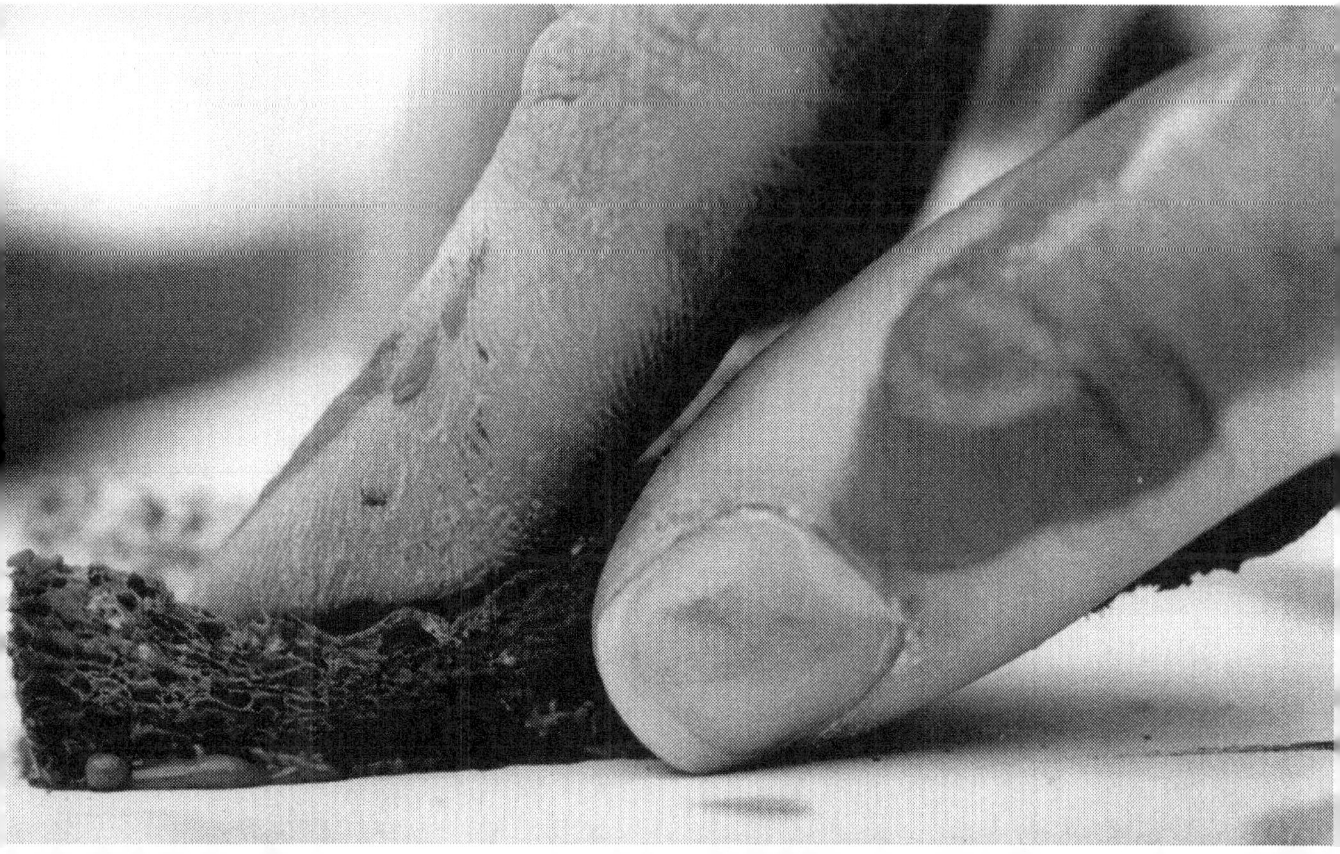

Times to Remember

By Julia Erratt
Music and Theatre Conservatory

Six long years are finally coming to an end. It is hard to imagine life without OCHSA—the singing on the stairwells and smiling faces, not only from the students but also the faculty. These past six years have been filled with the most amazing experiences of my life. When I made the decision to attend OCHSA at the end of my sixth grade year, I knew that I was leaving my friends and that I had a new future ahead of me. Yet graduation still seemed so far away. As I look back, these six years have gone by faster than I ever could have imagined. I have met the most remarkable people at OCHSA, each one of them unique.

OCHSA has changed my life and helped me to realize my strengths, weaknesses, and passions. It is said that we have created an "OCHSA family," and I cannot agree more. When you form a school with dedicated students who have a passion for the arts, it's an extraordinary result. As we come to the harsh realization that in a matter of months we will not have our "family," it is hard to comprehend. We have come to depend on one another. The initial reaction from other high school students is that our days are long, but when you are doing something you love, it is worth it. Friendships made at OCHSA will last a lifetime because these people have been there through the most challenging, as well as the brightest, moments of life.

What Makes a Beautiful Person?

By Nina Herzog
Music and Theatre Conservatory Class of 2009

It was a typical morning at the Orange County High School of the Arts (OCHSA). Our energetic literature teacher stood before the class invoking our imaginations by asking a thought provoking question: "What makes a beautiful person?"

"I want you guys to please tell me some of your ideas." These were the words that so often come from the mouths of teachers at OCHSA. Every one of them is truly interested in the opinions and feelings of their students, and each individual is heard and recognized.

"A beautiful person is someone who reaches out to make friends with the new kids," Erin said.

"Yes! Absolutely Erin!" said the teacher. "Anyone else have an idea?"

"A beautiful person is someone who isn't afraid to be their true self," Jade answered.

"Someone who cares for the environment," replied another student.

"Someone who loves to dance in the rain and sing in the halls!" shouted another.

As my peers around me became excitedly involved in this topic and every student chimed in with what they felt was a beautiful person, I sat back and looked around while a sudden realization came over me: Every characteristic that was mentioned could be found in the students around me. Every person that I had ever met at OCHSA really was a beautiful person, always reaching out to make new friends and forever caring for the environment. They were students who didn't think twice before dancing in the rain and who were never caught in the school hallways without a beautiful song passing through their vocal cords.

Jade's comment that a beautiful person is someone who isn't afraid to be their true self stuck with me. It seems to be the perfect phrase for summing up the essence of OCHSA.

OCHSA is a place where no matter your race, your style, or your sexuality, you can come to grow up and immediately be accepted by everyone around you. A beautiful person is someone who isn't afraid to be their true self, someone who reaches out to make new friends with the new kid, someone who saves the environment, and someone who dances in the rain and sings in the halls. A beautiful person is an OCHSA person.

The Emperor's New Clothes

By Andrew Aguilar
Music and Theatre Conservatory Class of 2009

I realized I loved acting when I auditioned in third grade for a school play "The Emperor's New Clothes." In preparing for this play, I worked hard memorizing lines and songs. I earned the lead part as the Emperor. When I performed the play and heard everyone cheering for me, I knew I wanted to be an actor. After that experience, I became involved with the Metropolitan Educational Theater. By sixth grade, I felt like I didn't quite fit in at my school because I was so small and scrawny. The other boys liked to play football, but I wasn't that good and was easily tackled. My interest wasn't sports, but theater. My mom and I began looking for a better school because my current school had a lot of mean cliques. We wanted to find a place where I could better myself. My mom gave me hope when she found out about a school for the arts called OCHSA. I applied and auditioned with Mr. Jeff Paul. When I found out I was accepted, I realized I had found my destiny.

Acting increases my self-esteem. I like to make people laugh. I hope that in the future I not only become a great actor, but also a great director. My seventh grade acting teacher, Mrs. Kent, made me feel special. In Mrs. Kent's showcase, I performed a comedy skit. I also found a manager. Since I've been at OCHSA, I feel special and fortunate because I have talented friends and a dream for my future. I feel so proud to be a student at OCHSA.

A New Beginning

By Courtney Symonds
Creative Writing Conservatory Class of 2008

My elementary school experience was average. Not outstanding, not awful, just average. I was a naturally quiet child. I spent a lot of my days on the playground by myself rather than playing sports with the popular kids. I was never athletic. I disliked sports because I was horrible at all of them. I enjoyed the time to myself, time to get lost in my own thoughts for twenty or thirty minutes, or however long recess lasted.

When I came to OCHSA in seventh grade, I came with the intention of starting fresh. I wanted to go to a place where no one knew me, a place I could finally be a butterfly, a place I could be completely different from the quiet child I used to be.

Four years later and I am pleased to say that I have made many wonderful friends. I've also met many of my closest friends at OCHSA. I am much more outgoing than I was back in elementary school, though I am still quiet and shy in a classroom setting. I love my wide variety of OCHSA friends and wouldn't trade them for anything.

I smile when my friends greet me with hugs each morning before class. It brings me just as much joy to see others being given a "good morning" hug from their friends. Nowadays, I am in a contented state of well being that opens my mind up to all possibilities, though I am still free to have and express my dislikes. I have a positive attitude that enables me to focus and excel academically and artistically. I'm so glad I chose to attend OCHSA! After attending this school, I could never go back to a traditional high school. I'd probably fall back into my shy, own little world. Now, I am still in my own little world at school, it's called OCHSA!

A Misunderstood Life

By Martha Rivera
Instrumental Music Conservatory Class of 2008

The students of the instrumental music class set up, moving stands and talking about how nerve-racking school life was. They had no idea how crazy it was to be in a school where nobody had the same goals or ideals. Where everyone's idea of success was to graduate from high school and not even consider college because it really wasn't an option. The only options we had were to work at McDonald's or get pregnant and live the life of an uneducated housewife with a husband who earned minimum wage. That was something I didn't even consider in fifth grade, or even now, when I know there is a whole world out there waiting for me.

In school it is impossible to not know anybody, so you could say I had friends. Here is this normal girl from Santa Ana, who has grown up in a city where gangsters and hip-hop are life, listening to Beethoven's "Eroica." Who would have thought that a girl who studied in the Santa Ana Unified School District could graduate junior high class valedictorian with a medal in music? My "friends" sure didn't. Everyone criticized my every move, even how I dressed. They especially didn't like how I knew more information on certain aspects of life usually reserved for "rich people." Something as simple as going to watch a symphony only fueled their idea that I was the class nerd and wanted to be the "white girl" in the class. I didn't know the respectable things like who the newest drug dealer was.

All the adults liked me for being different, but they didn't have to go through what I did every single day—getting fake smiles from people and my friends drifting away every day because, in reality, we had nothing in common. When they wanted to discuss how hot the new kid was, I was concentrating on reading a play by Shakespeare. Why would anybody read Shakespeare for fun? The only people that actually understood me were my mother and my flute teacher, Ana. They understood that music wasn't a way to show off, as a lot of my classmates often accused, but a way for me to express my emotions.

They were the pillars and the foundation that helped me get through school. But Ana had other plans. She strongly believed in me and gave me the encouragement I needed to think about auditioning for OCHSA. Who would have thought that the class nerd would try to get into a good school?

The weeks went by and I received my audition piece. Were they crazy? They wanted me to play the piece I had heard so many times before, but that I had never actually played, Beethoven's "Eroica." Hello! The hardest piece I had ever played had been an arrangement that Mr. V, my music teacher, had set. Now I had something to look forward to, spending two weeks in a room practicing for two hours. Amazing!

A Misunderstood Life

Two weeks in one room, this could not be fun. The hours quickly passed and yet nothing changed, I had to keep practicing. I had to prove to myself and to other people that I did have talent and that I wasn't just doing it to annoy (as they often accused).

The audition came and went—and boy was that stressful. The audition actually went well; I wasn't nervous at all. I heard people ahead of me, and they were amazing. I was pessimistic about my audition because, compared to other people, I wasn't that good. But I held on to my confidence. Two weeks later I received a letter congratulating me on being accepted to OCHSA. Yea! Who would have known that a single letter could change my life?

Since I've been at OCHSA, I have completely changed. During the first day of school my freshman year, I got smiled at so many times that I just had a natural impulse to smile at everyone around me, especially because I met Shannon McFarland. That girl can smile through the worst situations. I think some of it rubbed off on me. Here people weren't staring at me trying to find a flaw. They were welcoming me.

The first day of conservatory was pure bliss. Here I could talk about how I found certain recordings lacking or how I found a certain piece boring because it lacked emotion. People actually understood me! I had been accepted as I was without criticism or intimidation. OCHSA has been a place where I have come to understand how to live in a certain way. I find that I have a talent and that there is always room for improvement. Here, my friends are all different. That difference is what makes us all special.

A talent should not be something to be embarrassed about, but something that proves you different. I personally know how hard it is to not be normal, but here is the question: What is normal? Who defines normal? Every single human being has a different belief of what normal is. Are you normal? We shouldn't fall prey to what people believe. This is a valuable lesson I have learned at OCHSA. *Don't let people judge you. Be yourself.*

OCHSA has a great environment in which people work together. I have no idea how to work a saw, but here I am talking to my friend Krysten who is in the Production and Design Conservatory about her project for costume class. We don't need to be in the same conservatory to understand each other. Each of us is different, but we all have one common focus: art. No matter what form it may come in, we understand that each of us loves it and respects it, and that's what unites us.

A Magical Concert at Carnegie Hall

By Eunice Kim

Instrumental Music Conservatory Class of 2008

I grew up in Fullerton where I lived with my sister and parents. I had never moved. I grew up with girls and boys that had similar ethnic and cultural backgrounds as I did. I was in a secure layer of protection roaming my junior high years with my four best girlfriends. In addition, my older sister ruled high school; she was infamous throughout. I grew up around all her friends' protection, so entering my freshman year was a breeze. I had great times and memories throughout freshman year, attending every dance and every football game. I was living the true high school life. When I decided to transfer to OCHSA, I was assuming I would once again be comfortable with school.

My first day of school ended bleakly. I came home and serenely told my mother I wanted to be home-schooled and went to my room, shutting the door carefully. That was that. My mother disregarded every statement I had made about OCHSA, reminding me that it was my decision to attend. Months and months passed and I was barely eased of my uncomfortable school life. Finally, my conservatory's trip to New York was approaching and I was starting to get excited. I planned to room with my three closest friends that I had made at OCHSA: Alice, Rose, and Susie. I had the time of my life. Every day in New York was a dream. We performed a great concert at Carnegie Hall, ate at every moment we could spare, and I even attended my first Mets game!

The last day before we returned to Orange County, Mr. Russell, my conservatory director, gave a touching speech about how he appreciated our commitment and dedication to making this trip a success. I looked around the room and was amazed at the look I saw in every student's eyes. Mr. Russell had our full attention and gave us a great heart-wrenching speech. I realized the trip was too short.

The airplane ride back to California was a solemn experience. A myriad of students were glum at the thought of leaving the haven of New York. I was at a point of depression when we landed at LAX and had to part from each other. The trip brought us together and gave us a glimpse of a musician's hard but invigorating life. It was the best trip I had ever been on. I give Mr. Russell all of the credit for making the trip happen. Without his dedication, support, and impeccable commitment, the trip would not have been possible.

Mr. Russell has been one of the greatest things about OCHSA. At first I was befuddled as to why I had moved schools. After the New York trip and a year of studying with Mr. Russell, I have truly been able to realize that music is and always will be part of me. This year, Mr. Russell has given me the chance to lead my cello section in a wonderful season of symphonies. Even though I miss notes in my solo and turn beet red when the entire orchestra laughs, I thank Mr. Russell for always supporting me and giving me help when I need it. So, I would like to thank Mr. Russell and the rest of the orchestra for helping me discover my passion in life!

Photo by Ariel Lindquist, Visual Arts alumnus

The Universal Language

An Interview with Carol Green

Founding Board Member and Former Chair, Orange County High School of the Arts Foundation

Carol Green became involved with OCHSA after its second year. She has two children, both of whom attended OCHSA. Soon after her involvement, she joined the school's Foundation board. When Judy Sabbagh retired, Carol took her place as chair of the board.

Interviewer: *How did you first become aware of the Orange County High School of the Arts?*

Carol: I have a daughter who was a dancer. One of her instructors suggested she audition. That was the first I had heard of the school.

Interviewer: *Why did they suggest OCHSA? Was is just for the arts or was there another reason?*

Carol: I think because she really enjoyed dancing and she was bright. They wanted her to have a full experience and they knew OCHSA was a place where you she could get that full experience. The school provided strong academics, as well as excellent arts programs. A student like my daughter could get more exposure to all types of dancing and, also, strong academics.

Interviewer: *Are there other benefits to attending an arts school over a traditional school?*

Carol: I think it gives students training and exposure they're not able to get at other high schools. The academics and arts at OCHSA are wonderful, but I think it also gives them self-confidence and poise. These kids can go up and talk with anyone. It doesn't matter who they are. It's easy for them to have a conversation. They are self-assured. They're not afraid to go on a job interview. They're not afraid to say "I feel this is important, listen to me." OCHSA students learn that their feelings, thoughts, and ideas are important. I think it's a skill that so many people don't cultivate.

OCHSA offers a much broader education. My son graduated from UCLA in Theater Arts and one of the things he said was, "Mom, they really haven't taught me much more than I learned at OCHSA." So I

116

The Universal Language

think that that speaks well for our program when they're teaching at a level as high as college.

I also think that the arts are a universal language, so they helps kids understand other cultures. Through the arts I think they develop a better understanding of other people throughout the world, not just people like themselves.

Interviewer: *Your son also attended OCHSA. Was your family an artistic family to begin with?*

Carol: We enjoy the arts. I can't say that I'm terribly artistic, nor is my husband. But the kids have always enjoyed the arts, and we've always felt it's important for children, whether they're artistic or not, to be exposed to the arts. I believe that any child who has a desire to do some kind of art should be encouraged. It may not become their life's work, but allowing them to develop their talents is important. It enriches their growth. OCHSA also broadens the student's understanding and appreciation of all the arts—not just the one they intended to study.

Interviewer: *What was OCHSA like when you were first associated with it?*

Carol: OCHSA was like a family early on, because it was small. The parents, the board, faculty, everybody was really close. Everybody knew each other. We knew all the kids. All the students were kind of like our kids. We nurtured them; we were excited when any one of them did something special.

Interviewer: *What's the difference between OCHSA in its early years and now?*

Carol: For one thing, OCSHA is huge compared to what it was when my daughter graduated in 1992. Also, I think students and parents have a better perception of what the school is all about. Back then, it was pretty much unknown to the community. And many people thought of arts kids as being a little different, and that they wouldn't fit in with the football players and a lot of the other trappings of a traditional

The Universal Language

high school. However, the OCHSA kids proved them wrong and integrated into the school quite well, and I think helped develop a much greater understanding of the arts among the other students as well as the community in general.

Interviewer: *Can you relate a particular experience that somehow typifies or sums up the type of school OCHSA is?*

Carol: When my daughter was a junior she had a serious auto accident. She suffered major head injuries and broke almost every bone in her body. She wasn't expected to live or be normal. It was a long journey, but she came through it and is now perfectly healthy. She has since graduated from OCHSA and college. She's married and has a child. But back then, we couldn't see how it was all going to turn out. It was a trying time, to say the least.

I have to say OCHSA was a wonderful community. We spent many a day at the hospital. The accident didn't happen here, but when she was transferred to a local hospital most of my year was spent either going to the hospital or the rehab facility—and there was always somebody from the school who would come by to see us, both students and parents. They were there for us all the time.

After her rehab, OCHSA not only welcomed her back and gave her support, but helped her build her confidence. It takes a lot of poise and ability to put yourself out there after you've gone through an accident as traumatic as hers. She's been able to do that and I think OCHSA helped.

When it happened, our son was in a program that was slightly affiliated with OCHSA, but wasn't actually part of OCHSA. Many of the instructors were OCHSA students and they were all really good about making sure that he was being successful and that he was happy. That was tremendous because when we were away and he was here—it was difficult. But he was well supported and then later on he came to OCHSA as well.

Becoming Normal

By Allison Young
Instrumental Music Conservatory Class of 2009

I looked around me. There were new faces, familiar faces, faces I knew from elementary school, but no faces that knew more than my own face or my true self, my true thoughts and feelings. They saw my talent, intelligence, and my ethnicity. But did they see or care about my passion, my personality, or my hopes and dreams? No, I was much too deep, different, and quiet, to be recognized as one of the "normal" people in middle school.

The feeling of isolation led me to believe that I was too "special" to be a real person. I compared myself with the people who judged me, the people who didn't have goals in their lives other than being the most popular girl or guy on campus. At age 11, I auditioned and was accepted into a high school orchestra. Because I was constantly around older people who performed as well as me, I felt secluded. I longed to be like one of the "normal" people sitting around me all the time; I wanted to feel accepted.

At the time, I didn't realize that I *was* normal; I was at the level I was supposed to be at for playing the violin. I wasn't aware of the musical society or the many violin players that, at the time, were just like me. As a consequence, my passion, skill, and motivation for the violin gradually deteriorated. I was going to quit the violin forever because I felt so alone. But, my parents, my family, and my hope pulled me through.

In eighth grade, after I was accepted into the Orange County High School of the Arts, I realized that there were other children like me. I gradually began to let my inner self go and allow other people see the real me. I rediscovered the long forgotten love I felt every time I picked up my violin. I felt the energy and the emotions that flowed from my heart into the music I created. I made new friends and I met new faces—faces that knew me and cared about me, regardless of my differences. In return, I also began to care for people who were outside of my social status in middle school. I especially cared for the new kids at school. I knew what it felt like to be left alone because you're different, or when you are thrust into a new place with so many new faces.

OCHSA has taught me the importance of laughter and friends, the importance of an open mind, and the importance of having a dream, an aspiration, and a light at the end of the tunnel. The Orange County High School of the Arts has not only healed my mind, my music, and my self-perception, but it also healed my heart and my attitude toward life.

Healer's Music

By Janet Lee
Instrumental Music Conservatory Class of 2008

"Go on. Play it for me honey. I know you can," she said encouragingly. Her chapped right hand, which has been withered with age, seemed to pause in motion, anticipating what I'd do next. Her breath, with a hint of peppermint, blew dreams and hopes up my spine, sending mixed messages of doubt into my head. I smiled up at her beautiful, yet melancholy face. Wrinkles arched over her eyes in an attempt to shade her from reality and worries. *What makes her so down?* I once thought. I stared down at my hands. *If the notes ring upon my command, will that cure her?* I'd like to find out.

With numerous attempts to create a somewhat acceptable "peace on earth" for my dear friend, my glance found her in mid-trance, dazed. She was too far away to retrieve again with my small vulnerable hand. I watched. "We'll do it all. Everything you'd ever want. Sweetie, don't give up. Someday…." She outstretched her hand to push strands of my hair back to see my face clearly. She did not like what she saw—fear. Reminiscing, a curtain of shadow drew across her face. I couldn't see her. My grandmother.

Years passed and my portrait was reflected on the window pane of my mom's old Mazda SUV. My heartstring pulled, straightening my smiling face when I noticed something else I had not seen in such a long time—that weary smile of my friend, my grandmother. I looked up at the beautiful checkered clouds in the sky to feel her aura near me once again, but with no such luck.

As I looked at my reflection in the car window, I thanked God for leaving small remnants of my grandmother in my facial structure. Suddenly, my mom's head jerked toward a foreign seven-story building. I realized that we had finally arrived at OCHSA.

My digression interfered with my mental practice mode. *E, A, then G, not A#, B, then G. Get it right Janet.* As I talked to myself, the notes from the piece I memorized flew out from my brain. All my effort vanished through the thin smoke of bewilderment. Peering through the stained window, it took me a while to process that I was there for my audition. My mom and I got out of the car silently, avoiding each other's glance so as to not show any feelings of self-doubt. While my unworn black dress shoes glided easily along the pavement with the help of the sureness of my stride, my mom was only able to somewhat mimic my fake self-confidence as she traced the shadow lurking behind me. When I gazed back at my shadow, it seemed to be hesitant to follow my footsteps into the building. I braced myself to enter.

Room 201 was our destination. The elevator's inner decoration shocked my mom and me. We couldn't help but giggle at the tawdry floral carpeting engulfing us. And all this time we thought my grandmother's fashion sense needed some critiques. The elevator squeaked lazily open on the fourth floor, and we escaped its mechanical mouth of doom. We promised to take the stairs on our way down. The hallways were parallel to one

Healer's Music

another; hostile Xeroxed arrows beckoned us to the end of the mile-long stretch where life forms were actually heard: the screeching of violins, the chatter of nervous kids and caffeine-driven mothers, and those just standing quietly by. I had an excruciating fifteen minutes before I had to put on my game face and get the nerve-racking audition over with.

"Janet. Janet Lee. We're ready for you," a man in a black suit called for me through a crack in the door. The man introduced himself as Mr. Russell, Instrumental Music Conservatory director. Entering into the cold, condensed room, I realized he wasn't the only judge. Behind a long polished oak table sat a jolly old man about the age of 45, curling his already curled hair around his stubby index finger, looking toward my direction. His spectacles reminded me of Harry Potter and fascinated me when I saw his kind, plump face near Mr. Russell's prim, proper, and stiff suit. For a brief second, I found this comical and felt comforted by my own humor. It was one of the oddest moments in my entire life, because the audition process in my memory was blank, like a roll of film exposed too early to the light, erasing captured images, all vanished. All that I could have recalled was the jolly man's Hawaiian shirt shaking with his uneasy intake of breaths, and Mr. Russell looking at my profile to comment, "Happy Birthday tomorrow Janet." With the last second of awkward silence, I left the building with my mom, violin trembling in my hands.

I first felt ambivalent to find out my successful audition results in June. I enjoyed performing as a hobby, but never seriously considered risking my valuable time in music; I was hoping for something else in my future.

I still ask myself why I chose to go. The answer is I chose to go to commemorate my dearest grandmother and her passion. Even while she continuously battled her incurable disease, music soothed her and allowed her to appreciate, to reconfirm why she still existed. She struggled with depression every day of her life after she realized she was captured by Alzheimer's disease, forgetting the fondest people in her life. Music was what delayed and bought her time from this particular disease; she would not remember my name, but would remember each music piece we had shared. There were secret codes encrypted between her and I to meet each other and reintroduce ourselves before she would be overwhelmed with too much information to forget again. It scared her. Even I understood that at such an early age.

Violin performance will not be my career, but through learning music at OCHSA I am planning to become a psychologist, focusing on incorporating music therapy to help those struggling with autism, Alzheimer's, and depression. People can be cured from, or at least delay, the ravages of mental illnesses. I like knowing that I have provided a little comfort to my grandmother before she passed away; I hope to help others in similar situations. Being trapped inside of one's own thoughts isolates one from reality, and music may be the only solution to carry one back to safety and the real world. I couldn't see my grandmother before, but now I can always see parts of her through music.

"Bemoaning Lost Love"

By Lisa Meyers
Creative Writing Conservatory Class of 2007

My relevance to you is spoiled like milk

On kitchen counter of your disregard

And I, like tragic heroes of my ilk,

Sit stalwart on my couch, moan life is hard

To say you occupy my heart's whole hell

Is like to introduce my nose to face

"With this, dear friend, I sniffle, breathe, and smell."

(So blatantly I'm barren of your grace)

And thus I curdle, Kleenex, kvetch, and crow

Watch Sleepless in Seattle just to feel

Drink bitterness-spiced Coke and cookie dough

And let my higher hemispheres congeal

To lapse in love does not equate to hate

But weren't I worth it to refrigerate?

THE RESULT

*"I could be bounded a nutshell,
and count myself a king of infinite space"*

--HAMLET, WILLIAM SHAKESPEARE

Landscape by Marie Breyfogle, Visual Arts alumna

The Singing Soccer Player

An interview with Cindy Boragno
Orange County High School of the Arts Parent and President of ENCORE!

I've always had a unique child in that since he was about three years old, he was always singing—primarily classical music. Growing up in a sports-driven world is not easy for a young boy who wants to sing classical music. He used to play soccer. He was the only player on the soccer field singing little arias. Of course, we didn't know they were little arias at the time. All of his friends would say, "Nicholas, stop singing and kick the ball." He was actually a pretty good soccer player, but he never stopped singing.

Nicholas became captivated by classical music when he heard it on the radio. One of his teachers recognized his unique gift for music and encouraged him to enroll in voice lessons. Nicholas began collecting classical music CDs—he probably has over 300 or 400 CDs at this time. As Nicholas advanced in school, he continued to sing, but the other kids didn't always understand his passion or where he was coming from. His peers didn't understand why anybody would want to sing classical music—or sing at all.

I was called into school on a number of occasions because he was singing in class. And while his singing in class was inappropriate, I felt it could have been handled differently. Nicholas had always been a top student, but his grades began to drop. He was just . . . well, he was changing, and he wasn't feeling good about himself. As his mother, I knew I needed to do something to improve his situation.

I heard about the Orange County High School of the Arts through friends. Nicholas needed a safe haven that would allow him to develop his talents. He found that safe haven at the Orange County High School of the Arts. He found a place where students are accepted and revered for their talents. In fact, his former school has invited him to come speak to students about the arts on several occasions. Now he hears kids saying "I hope I can be like Nicholas one day."

During his studies at the Orange County High School of the Arts, Nicholas has become a passionate and driven young man who knows what his future holds in store for him. He knows that he wants to be a professional opera singer one day. He knows that he wants to sing in the best concert houses in the world. He lives, eats, and breathes opera day in and day out. He has no question in his mind and that the Orange County High School of the Arts has given him the ability to pursue his dream.

Cindy Boragno has been involved with the Orange County High School of the Arts for the past six years and serves as the current president of ENCORE!, one of the school's support groups. She also served as the chair of Gala 2006. Her son, Nicholas Boragno, is currently a senior in the school's Opera Conservatory.

Finding Direction

By Candice M. Clasby
Music and Theatre Conservatory Class of 2002

When I first started at OCHSA, I was a sophomore and the school was still part of Los Alamitos High School. My focus at the time was voice, but as the years progressed it grew more towards acting. When I was over at the new location in Santa Ana, I was still a vocal major but was somehow cast in the plays and not so much the musicals. But by the end of my senior year, it seemed that my life was going, yet again, in another direction—this time towards directing.

It was part of our senior project to either buy the rights to a show or write our own and perform it in Symphony Hall. We had to do everything from finding people to work the show, to reserving the space for the night and for rehearsals, to scheduling our own rehearsals. Luckily we could rehearse during class time. Our section of the class opted to perform an original work. They also opted that I write it. I insisted that if I were to write it, I would also get to direct it. All agreed.

When the show went up, there were a few flaws, as can be expected, but overall it went so well that I couldn't help but jump up and down.

It has been four years since I graduated from OCHSA. I am in my fifth and final year at Cal State University, Fullerton as a directing major. It started much the same way: I went in as a musical theatre hopeful, I became an acting major for a year, and I am now in the Advanced Directing Program.

It is true what they say about history repeating itself, but I like to think that OCHSA gave me my first hint at what I could do for a career. I have directed numerous scenes and have now been urged in to directing and choreography. I was assistant choreographer for *Cabaret* in spring 2006. Now I am co-choreographer for *Seussical,* which opens mid-October. In addition, I am directing my own one act and still performing on the side.

I am also trying to start up the West Coast Company of the Neo-Futurists, which perform *Too Much Light Makes the Baby Go Blind,* a show in which 30 plays are performed in a single hour. It started as a company in Chicago and now there's one in New York, but it has yet to hit the West coast. Having directing under my belt has broadened my opportunities to work in this industry. If I had been asked 10 years ago what I wanted to do, I would have told them I wanted to be a dancer, singer, or actor. But I also knew I wanted to work! And that's what I am doing. OCHSA gave me a base from where to start, and I know I wouldn't be doing what I am doing today if it weren't for the opportunities I had been given and the contacts I had made through OCHSA.

Stepping Out of My Comfort Zone

By Brittany Weston
Music and Theatre Conservatory Class of 2007

I was mortified. I had never done anything of the sort. I was new at the school and knew just about no one. I was not prepared to do this. I got up on stage, literally shaking, thinking "I am not doing this. I cannot do this." But something happened during that monologue. I became so emotionally involved in the role that I almost was not me anymore. When I was finished, I was shaking and completely flabbergasted with myself. I had stepped outside of myself and became another person entirely. It was from that point on that I realized I could act and that I actually loved doing so.

My teacher encouraged me to become involved in theater, yet I was still scared. Finally in my sophomore year I decided to leave the varsity dance team and try something new. I shared my love for theater arts with the community while performing *Cinderella, Seussical the Musical, U.S. Oh No!, Bye Bye Birdie, Grease,* and *Oklahoma.* I enjoyed theater, yet I felt like everything else in my life was stagnant. I felt completely unmoti-vated at school. It seemed that nobody else was zealous for life or the future, and this brought me down significantly. My school was filled to the brim with four thousand other adolescents, and everything felt so impersonal. Relationships with teachers were hard to attain because of the size of classes. It was practically impossible to know your entire class because of the size. Overall, it felt like going to school was a robotic motion and nothing else. I needed something to kick me forward, and that was when I made the decision to audition for OCHSA. I was ecstatic to find that a close friend and I had been accepted. In August of 2005, we took the forty-five minute train ride from Corona to Santa Ana for our first day of school.

We were blown away by the difference in our peers at OCHSA as opposed to our peers at our former school. We were attending school with people who chose to be there. We were at school with other kids who were passionate about something they were good at and who chose to stay at school until five o'clock every evening in order to pursue

Stepping Out of My Comfort Zone

their dreams. Almost immediately, things within me changed. I was excited about life. I cared about my future and loved staying three extra hours at school performing monologues and songs for an experienced staff that cared about my growth as a performer and a person. I wanted to be involved and audition and spend as much time growing with these teachers and students as I could.

In coming to OCHSA, I am able to be all of me. I can be enthusiastic about school because all of my peers are enthusiastic about school. I spend my days with a group of people who are not only passionate about the arts, but who are passionate about life. I walk down the halls and see someone in a tutu, someone playing guitar in a corner, and hear someone's operatic voice reverberate throughout the walls. The extra pressure of not only having academic homework, but having additional homework in acting class or having to prepare a song for musical theater voice class have made me more assertive and goal-oriented. People are in awe over the fact that I would go through so much effort to get to and from high school every day, but to me it is a given. The hour it takes to get to the station, take the train, catch the city bus, and then

walk the remainder of the way to get to school is more than worth it. I never thought that I would enjoy coming to school; not many can say that.

Making the decision to change my life significantly mid-high school career was probably one of the best things I have ever done for myself. Stepping out of my comfort zone time and time again has pushed me forward in all aspects of my life. I don't think I can say enough to describe how passionate I am about life, relationships, and memories. I have a list for miles of different things I want to try and different things I feel I need to do in this lifetime. I am zealous for life and living it to the fullest. I think that much of this passion can be attributed to the environment of my school and the passion that surrounds me every single day. Whether or not I become an actress, a business woman, or a teacher, I feel I have the tools to do it whole-heartedly and with fervor.

Dedication

By Fallon Geiger
Commercial Dance Conservatory Class of 2008

Can you see yourself waking up every morning, five days a week, at five a.m.? Taking a train to school and back, staying late almost every night for extracurricular activities, and staying up until early hours in the morning finishing homework all describe the life of a dedicated OCHSA student.

For the past three years I have had the same routine every day and I never seem to become tired of it. The first impression I get from people when I tell them I go to high school in Orange County is, "Why the heck are you doing that?" I tell them that not only am I receiving a great education, but also every day I get to do what I love the most—dance.

Ever since I was young, I have not been able to sit still while listening to music. Even as a baby I would not go to sleep unless my little radio was on in my room. My mom signed me up for dance classes since I would not sit still—and to try to make me feel important when my younger sister was born. Ever since then, my passion for dance has skyrocketed. I am now getting training from amazing teachers. I have won numerous awards and scholarships, and have already been signed to an agency and have begun to build my resume. I am well on my way to pursuing a career in the dance industry.

Although dance has always been my number one choice for a career, I have always shown a strong passion for the medical field. Then, one day I thought, "Why can't I combine the two careers to make something unique and special to me?" In my years of being a dancer, I have suffered many injuries and actually went to physical therapy for a problem I had with my knees. My physical therapist was able to rehabilitate my knee. However, he didn't have lot of knowledge of dance and wasn't able to understand where I was coming from. So, with my extensive knowledge of the body and dance, and my strong passion in the medical field, I now want to become a dance physical therapist.

I took my first college course this summer, from which I learned a lot. Through my education at OCHSA, I have learned that nothing can be accomplished without strong motivation and determination.

As I move forward with my life, I know dance will always have a special place in my heart and I will never give it up. It is my passion, my reason for everything I do in life, my motivation. In the next couple of weeks, months, years, I could completely change what I want to do with my life. No matter what, I know that whatever I do—whether it be becoming famous, opening my own dance studio, or becoming a dance physical therapist—I hope to inspire someone the way my teachers inspired me. I hope to help someone accomplish and reach the goals they have set and to spark that fire and passion in their heart for dance so that they too can pass on that intensity and drive to someone else.

Happy In the Dungeon

By Kim Jones
Production and Design Conservatory Faculty

When I was first asked to begin instructing at OCHSA, I was thrilled at the idea of creating a program for students to learn about costuming. You see, as the first Costume Design instructor that the school ever had, I was excited at the prospect of pioneering a whole new program for the Production and Design Conservatory.

I began with little in the way of space to teach and materials and equipment to use, but I had ambition to spare. I was determined to teach even without the basics (namely sewing machines, books, fabrics, notions, and anything else that related to my field). Needless to say, the first few years at Los Alamitos High School were challenging at best.

My classroom was in the theater. Well, actually it was any part of the theater that wasn't being used by someone else at that time. Most of the time we were in one of the theater dressing rooms, but there was the odd occasion when we had to relocate due to a show. (Actually, that happened quite frequently as we did many productions throughout the year.) My students were quite adaptable, though, and we all muddled through.

I begged, borrowed, and pleaded for sewing machines, fabrics, notions, and any other items that I could use in my daily efforts. I am proud to say that through the years we have acquired 12 sewing machines, tons of fabrics, several cutting tables, and even a real classroom/lab to work in!

When I work in professional theaters, most of the wardrobe rooms are located in what we affectionately call "The Dungeon" or somewhere downstairs in the "bowels of the building," so it is almost poetic that our classroom is in the basement. Much to everyone's surprise, I was excited when I found out that was where we'd be. I feel right at home in the dungeon!

I still beg, borrow, and plead for fabrics, notions, and patterns. I never turn down any donation from any conservatory. Some things never change. We even have a mannequin now. We call her Trixie. I am proud to say that I have quite a few working graduates in the field. (You Go Guys!!!) Isn't it amazing what a little vision can accomplish?

Thanks, Ralph, for your vision so long ago to create a school for performing arts kids. Thanks to the great staff and faculty of this school. I'm proud and honored to be counted amongst you! And finally, thanks to all my great students. Keep reaching for your dreams and fly high, because you never know where you'll land!

Painting by Samantha Ryder, Visual Arts student

Life is Beautiful

By Jamie Schenk

Music and Theatre Conservatory Class of 2009

One might assume that students who choose to attend the Orange County High School of the Arts intend to pursue a career in their artistic specialty. Since I attend classes in the drama division of the Music and Theatre Conservatory, people might assume that I plan to become an actor whose biggest dream is to earn an Oscar or have a lead role in the Broadway production of *The Phantom of the Opera.*

However, it is entirely different with me. Fascinated with the medical world, my ultimate dream is to be a dermatologist. How could dermatology and acting possibly relate to each other? Acting has shown me the richness of life. Life is beautiful when you try new things. Acting has taught me to embrace life as it comes. Most importantly, acting has given me the confidence to pursue my dreams.

As a young girl, I would hide behind my mother's leg to avoid any social contact; talking felt intimidating to me, so I tried to do it as little as possible. When I was just seven years old, my mom enrolled me and my brother, Dave, in summer theater camp. At the end of the camp, we performed in *The Wizard of Oz* at Aliso Niguel High School and at the Crown Valley Regional Park. When I first walked on stage on opening night, I felt invincible. Those bright lights shining on my face as I sang, danced, and cheered made me feel like I was on top of the world. After the show was over, I had the indescribable feeling that I could accomplish whatever I set my heart to.

That first performance gave me a desire to recapture that unbelievable feeling. In third grade I, along with my mom and six other GATE students, joined Destination Imagination (DI). This non-profit organization blends academics with theater and creativity with homework. Our Team Tsunami won the regional competition three years in a row and in 2002 captured the California state championship. Our fifth grade team traveled to the University of Tennessee in Knoxville for the World DI Competition. Competing against teams from all over the country and from far off places including Honduras, Korea, and Peru gave me the confidence that I could compete at any level.

At age 13, I discovered the Orange County High School of the Arts. My older brother was a Film and Television Conservatory student. I attended the auditioning classes on Saturday mornings and applied to OCHSA that spring. Although I have absorbed so much by attending conservatory, I have grown the most as an individual during the academic day. The most amazing thing OCHSA has taught me is acceptance. As cliché as it sounds, I have learned to not judge a book by its cover. Under that cover we may find amazing stories. It is the same with people. Gaining so much as an individual has made me want to give these gifts to others.

All of the skills I have obtained through acting and OCHSA will ensure that my dream of being a dermatologist will become a reality. Reaching my goals will take confidence, a driven attitude, and problem-solving skills. Thanks to acting, I feel like such an amazing, intelligent, outgoing, and worldly person.

The Pianist

By Justin Lee

Instrumental Music Conservatory Class of 2011

The orchestra was getting ready for the Christmas concert. Mr. Mazur, the conductor, was conducting the tempo incredibly fast. I was in the cello section trying to keep up. The members of the orchestra were getting serious. The pressure was on. The concert was three weeks away. Mr. Kamida, the assistant conductor, then stepped into the rehearsal hall and made an announcement. There was no pianist for the concert because the pianist was ill and had been admitted to the hospital. The pianist was to be featured in the concert with the orchestra. Mr. Kamida asked for a volunteer to take the place of the hospitalized pianist.

Although I played piano for six years, I wasn't interested in volunteering because I had my own personal problems. I had always had a difficult time expressing myself with words. I had so many different feelings inside of me, but I couldn't put them into words. A few weeks prior to this incident I had changed piano teachers. My new teacher told me, "A piano is nothing but a piece of furniture. It's the person behind it that makes it come alive." After I had thought about it, I knew there was truth to that statement. I started to use the piano to express myself.

Suddenly, I put two and two together: Why not volunteer? The orchestra tuned up and then the announcement was made. I strode onto the stage and took my place at the piano. I waited for the conductor's downbeat. The members of the orchestra started to play. I came in and then let the feelings inside of me come out. The music was beautiful. I felt great. After the song, I took a bow. I had I met the challenge. At that moment and forever after, music had become a deep part of me.

Two Roads

By Tara Filowitz
Class of 1997

After graduating from OCHSA in 1997, I went east to Brandeis University and pursued a degree in theatre arts. From there, I went on to do several productions and moved out to New York City for a year to try my hand at the acting game. However, I suffer from Crohn's disease. The acting wasn't working out with the disease, so I had to rethink things.

Fortunately, before moving out to NYC, I had the opportunity to do some teaching at OCHSA. Working in the Integrated Arts / Music and Theatre Conservatories inspired me to look into the field of education. So, nearly 10 years later, OCHSA has led me to both of my careers—teacher by day and actress by night—and I am now close to finishing my master's in education at Chapman University.

OCHSA gave me wonderful friends whom I still love tremendously and keep in touch with. OCHSA gave me a sense of direction in multiple stages of my life. Now when they're looking to hire new teachers, they can look my way!

The Moment of Truth

By Cinthia Do
Visual Arts Conservatory Class of 2008

The first time I stepped onto the OCHSA campus was around April 2002 for my Visual Arts Conservatory audition. I was terrified. The moment I stepped into the classroom, I felt as if thousands of eyes were looking at me, analyzing me and ridiculing me. Truthfully, though, no one looked over at me with disdain because, well, no one ever looked at me.

I handed my portfolio to Paige, the ever-smiling Visual Arts Conservatory director, and with a weak smile quickly sat next to my friend. For about a year, I had trained and groomed for this moment. I spent hours drawing until my hands cramped and my pencil dulled. This was THE moment of truth. I was fairly confident—who wouldn't be after practicing for one audition for close to a year—but I felt my confidence waver as I looked at other students' drawings. Look at that color! Look at those strokes! I looked down at my own pitiful picture; I saw ordinary and out of proportion. I walked into my audition terrified, but with confidence. I left my audition with a sense of resigned failure. I felt as if all those months, days, hours, and minutes I spent drawing were all wasted. I wanted to crawl under a table and cry.

A month later, I received my letter from OCHSA. My mother barged into my room (scaring 10 years off of my life) with the acceptance letter in her hand. After celebrating my acceptance, I did a boogey dance while my mother smiled and laughed. I remember being surprised that I was accepted. Did the past months of working on my artistic skills pay off? Did they pick me because I was runner up? Did my amazing artistic skills strike their souls and brighten their lives? I doubted it, but I didn't care because not only did I get into OCHSA, but my best friend got in as well. This just made my victory of getting accepted so much sweeter.

My first day as a scrub (high school jargon for freshman) was as every scrub's first day should be: pee-my-pants terrifying. Meeting new teachers, being introduced to new students—it didn't matter that the other seventh graders were new like I was. Going to a new school was still terrifying. My first encounter with the never-ending malicious stairs scared me. I barely came out of the treacherous journey alive. The only time I was free from those stairs was during lunch. Lunch was pleasant not only because it involved no stairs, but also because I was in the company of my best friend and some new friends.

My favorite time of all, besides lunch, was conservatory. This was the time when I was surrounded by other students of my kind and was able to do what I had come to OCHSA to do. The knowledge that we were all new, including the teachers, was enough to calm my mind and unknot my stomach.

Now, I'm not one of those individuals who needs to draw to survive. Drawing to me is simply a hobby and something for which I have a knack. OCHSA is a place where I can draw to escape boredom. The school makes me feel accepted per se, and its ambience makes me feel comfortable. Though I am reluctant to leave OCHSA, I feel like I have to in order to learn more and to become more aware of the world. All in all, OCHSA has given me confidence and new friends, all of which I know I will have throughout my life.

Theatrical Changes

By Javier Lacayo
Music and Theatre Conservatory Class of 2008

Every person in this world has a defining figure, event, or passion in his or her life that shapes who they become, making a deep, everlasting impression in their lives. I have been in theater for five years. I have been through terrible disappointment and amazing success. Through my experiences, I have changed more than I could have imagined. Theater has been the driving force in my transformation from a timid little kid to a confident young man.

I remember the terrible feeling of insecurity I had as a child. I remember not liking myself when I was younger because I was never the best at sports. When everyone wanted to play kickball, I would find somewhere else to go in order to get out of playing the game. At times, I would purposely not dress up for P.E. because I was embarrassed by my lack of athleticism. I would go from hobby to hobby, desperately trying to fill an empty void that I could not find the root of. And then, one day in June, my life changed and that void was finally filled.

I did my first theater show the summer before sixth grade. When I returned to school that September, I was a new kid. I ran for student council and actually won. I made new friends and made a reputation for myself of being loud and outspoken. My laugh became the loudest in the room. The little boy who kept to himself and never talked to anyone was gone. This energy continued to get stronger.

As the years passed, I did more shows and also faced many rejections. But I grew from every experience. Theater helped me through one of the most awkward times in my —life—starting high school. Instead of being shy and scared, I walked into high school with a confident presence and quickly made friends. I was happy with myself and it showed.

Theater continues to steer the direction my life takes. It drove me to leave my old life and school and start a completely new life at OCHSA halfway through my high school career. Here, more than anywhere else, I feel accepted. Being in a world where football is not the priority is a big change for me. I have art to thank for that.

From the first time I stepped onstage, I knew that theater was what I had to do for the rest of my life. However, I had no idea how much it would change me as a person. My journey has been a crazy one, which no essay can summarize. My journey is also one that is far from over. I continue to change and grow due to theater. Where theater will lead me is still unknown. No matter where it takes me, I will always carry and treasure the impact that it has made on my life. Everyone has a defining figure, event, or passion in his or her life; mine is theater.

How OCHSA Has Affected My Life

By Warren Hagerty
Instrumental Music Conservatory Class of 2009

I'm not exactly sure what I want to do for a living. I enjoy what I do at OCHSA, but I don't look at the arts as an area in which I want to pursue a career. I have learned some valuable things at OCHSA, mostly having to do with creativity and being myself. I will incorporate many of them into my future career. OCHSA has made me see the world in a different way. It has helped me to better understand people who are different than me. No matter how strange someone may seem to me, I understand now that everyone is unique and that they each have their own motivation. It doesn't seem strange to me anymore being surrounded by black sheep. I think that will be a valuable way to look at life as I grow older.

Photo by Michael Richards, Visual Arts student

Standing in My Own Shoes

By Taylor Phillips

Integrated Arts Conservatory Class of 2011

Popular isn't everything. Being popular is anything *but* my goal in life. I don't pay attention to who's popular or not. But if you look at popular as a role based on how rich, pretty, or high class someone is, then it's practically as bad as judging someone's personality based on how they look.

My experience at an elementary private school wasn't the smoothest ride. Like a lot of my peers, I had a couple of great friends, and then I had my enemies. Although I was closer to my friends, my enemies were the ones who really stood out to me and made me realize who I was. They were the popular girls who didn't deserve the title of being "popular." They also made me realize who I didn't want to be and how I wasn't going to act.

Almost every day on the way home from school, I would talk to my mother about the negative people at my school and their behavior. She would tell me to stop looking at the bad actions and notice my friends, who *are* worth looking up to. And although I didn't notice it, when I got home I would crank up my stereo during homework time and bedtime. Whenever I would try to fall asleep at night, I would recollect the day's events, listening to music while doing so helped me to see different sides of the situation.

Subconsciously, I realized music had an enormous effect on me and how I looked at things, so I decided to give singing a chance. It has taken over a huge chunk of my heart. When I work on projects in class, I've found that listening to my iPod lets me zoom in and focus. If I'm not listening to music, I feel required to talk to other people about what the popular girls think about something, and that's not what life is about. Life is about discovering who *you* are and who you are going to be, not who someone else is or who they want to be.

Singing for a career was starting to come to the forefront of my thoughts by the end of sixth grade. When my mom told me about OCHSA, I knew it was where I wanted to go to school. I knew that it could open many doors for me, so it was practically a no-brainer. I was accepted for an audition, and it was uphill from there.

At first, OCHSA was lonely without my buddies, but I soon found one of my most sensitive, caring friends of all time, Jasmin. She could make me laugh no matter how down I was. About halfway through my seventh grade year at OCHSA, I heard about some current teen stars that had gone to the school. So I asked my mother if she would consider allowing me to audition for commercials. She told me there were a lot of tasks to be done, so I thought it would be something that

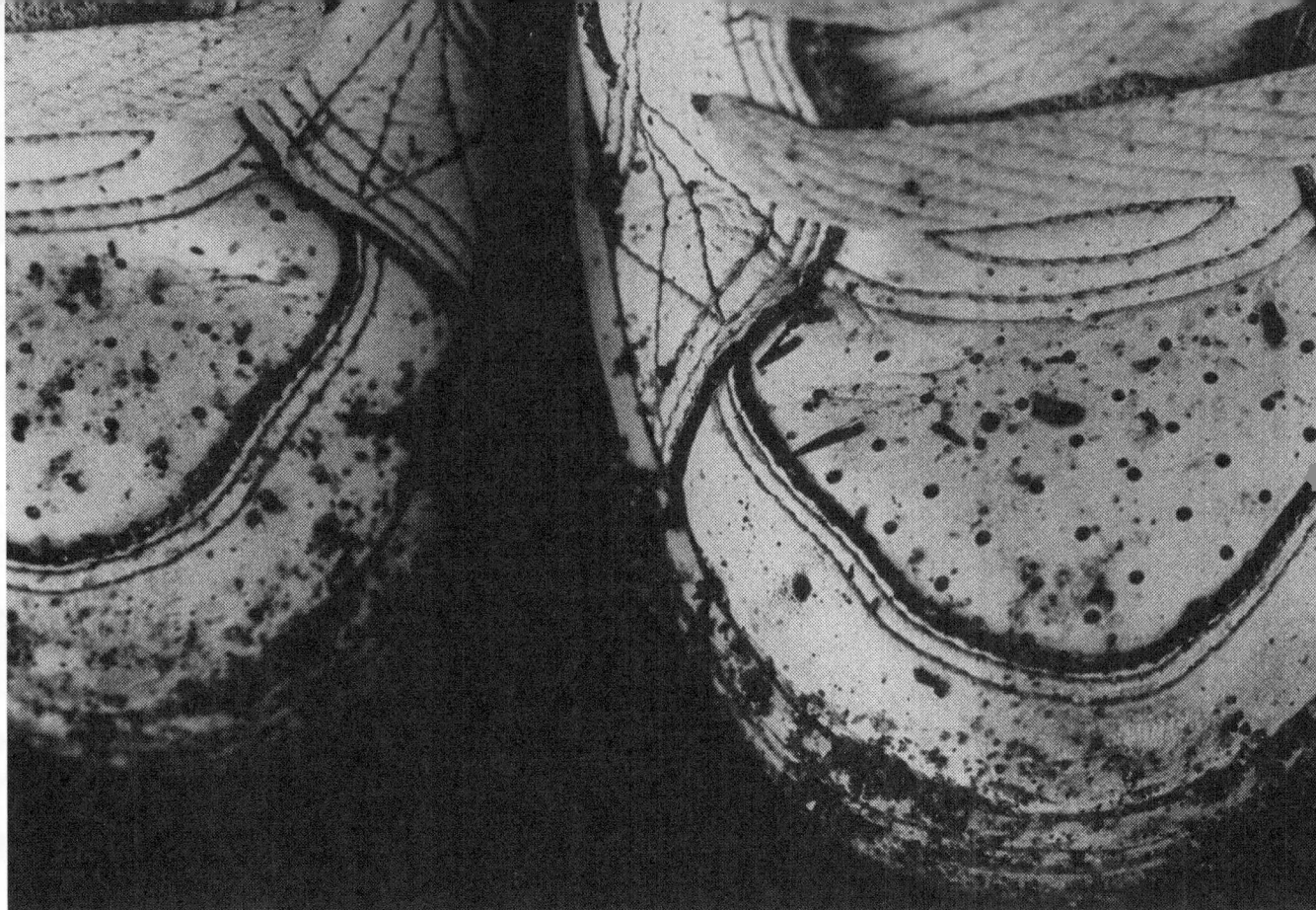

Photo by Mary Amor, Visual Arts alumna

Standing in My Own Shoes

we would talk about and then forget. Turns out it wasn't. We created a résumé, headshot, and all the other requirements for me to begin in show business.

I was recently in a commercial for a computer eyewitness product, and since then I've been busy almost every weekend with some kind of audition. I've also kept up with my pop vocal skills, and I practice every night (and every time I take a shower).

I've realized the reason I connect with the

songs I choose to sing is because I can open up as if I am writing in a journal. With acting it is the exact opposite. I enjoy it because it lets me step into someone else's shoes and forget about my problems and relax. So although popular people were what I hated the most, they helped me realize parts of personality that I would not have realized otherwise. And for that, I would like to thank them.

A Calling

An Interview with Cindy Peca
Assistant Director, Commercial Dance Conservatory

I started dancing professionally when I was seven and a half—I had been recognized by a talent scout when I seven. I worked professionally a lot between the ages of 7 and 18. I had a long-spanning career, working with the likes of Bob Fosse, Bob Hope, Rita Moreno, Tina Turner, Merv Griffin, Dick Clark, and Francis Ford Coppola.

At 15, I was at the top of my game and I felt everything was going my way; I was doing great in my career. At 16, I was asked to travel and study with Bob Fosse. My mom took me. My dad stayed behind to run the dance studio that we owned in Huntington Beach. Someone had to make a living while we went off on our great adventure!

Three years later, I was taking class at Steps on 74th. I did a grande battement and landed in a forced arch relevé. My kneecap shot behind my leg and shattered into three pieces. I woke up from emergency surgery to find that my dance career was on its way down; no longer would I be a professional dancer.

I had to find something else to do in my life. Well, there was no way I was going to let dance go, so I continued to teach. I was struggling with emotion, obviously, at the disappointment in my life. When I found out that I was no longer going to dance as I once did, I was filled with determination to find another way to make it through this world and still have dance in my life. I had no idea how I was going to do it, but I knew that I would do it. I was already teaching at my dance studio at the time, but I didn't feel that was my calling in life. I felt I was more of a performer.

When I was 19, I was offered a part-time teaching position at OCHSA. It was an opportunity to work with amazingly talented kids. I taught part-time in the Commercial Dance Conservatory and that progressed over the years until I was teaching full-time. I worked for the school for 11 years. It was located at Los Alamitos High School. I then traveled to the new site in Santa Ana where I became the assistant director of the Commercial Dance Conservatory under the direction of Jim Kolb. I was also doing most of the school-wide choreography at the time with David Green, who was in charge of all of the outside events.

A Calling

At 21, I was still in a state of confusion and shock. I didn't know why it had happened to me, this devastating injury. I loved performing so much. I was still teaching when one day, I was about 24, it hit me: this is my calling. My calling was to be a teacher at OCHSA, to be a mentor, to be a professional teaching my experiences, to teach and give my knowledge to these aspiring students.

Since then, I have tried to teach not only technique, but *proper* technique to these kids, the technique they need to keep their bodies healthy and to stay on top of their game, physically. The world of dance is ever-changing; it's evolving all the time. But, I also try to teach them life skills so that if they do fall upon an injury like mine, or if they have a different type of change in their life—something as simple as having children or getting married—they'll have what it takes to be successful in whatever they choose, to be able to handle rejection with grace and resilience, to face life as a learning experience and grow from it, and to be willing to be nurtured and to be nurturing.

Altogether, I'd say that my work here at OCHSA and what I've given to the school and the students is minimal compared to what OCHSA has given back to me. OCHSA has changed my life. I believe it is my calling. It gave me a place. It nurtured me when I needed nurturing. It also embraced me when I needed embracing. It encouraged me, it challenged me, and it inspired me. The students with their love and their desire to learn, the parents with their graciousness and care, the entire staff with their appreciation and passion for the arts, the board members with their thoughtfulness and insights, have all been amazing. Because of OCHSA, my life is much richer than it was 20 years ago—even with a wonderful career as a dancer. This is my life now; this is my career.

Making a Difference

An Interview with Heather Stafford
Director, Integrated Arts Conservatory

Heather: I am Heather Stafford, director of the Integrated Arts Conservatory, which is now in its third year at the Orange County High School of the Arts. I also teach the senior acting class in the music and theatre conservatory. I started at OCHSA in 1994 teaching ninth grade acting. Since then, I have taught seventh to 12th grade in various years and several different classes, including Shakespeare, Acting Styles, and Make-up.

Interviewer: *What exactly is Integrated Arts?*

Heather: The Integrated Arts Conservatory is designed for the young person, who is not sure what specific conservatory they want to pursue. They like to write, they like to sing and dance, they like to do visual arts. Quite often, the auditioning student is not happy in their neighborhood school. These talented young people are looking and needing something else —you sense that they have a passion for the arts and that passion is not being satisfied. OCHSA draws that passion out, and then directs and nourishes them to reach their artistic goals.

Integrated Arts gives them a diverse curriculum that includes, voice, acting, Musical Theatre, Film and Television, Creative Writing, Production and Design, Visual Arts, Stage Combat and Dance. The tenth grade will add a class in graphic arts and pop vocal. When they feel they want to change conservatories, they can make an informed decision about what department they want to pursue. If, however, they choose to stay in Integrated Arts, the plan for the future is to continue to the 12th grade.

Interviewer: *So what do you think brings these students to OCHSA?*

Heather: They sometimes have a neighbor who attends the school, they may hear about the school in their dance studio, they may go online and pursue their own audition and make their parents take them—there are a lot of different ways and a lot of different kinds of young people, but they all have a passion for the arts and a strong desire to be here.

Making a Difference

Interviewer: *In your professional career you've worked with a lot of actors that have come from major universities and all kinds of different programs. Is there an advantage to starting this young?*

Heather: The advantage of starting so young at OCHSA is that these kids are already focused, they're super high achievers. They want to go to NYU, they want to go to Carnegie-Mellon, they want to go to USC, and they want to go to the good schools. Their résumés look a lot better when they have all these conservatory classes behind them. Besides, the school is excellent, academically. We have a lot of AP classes. The academic staff here is excellent about supporting the arts. It's a great environment for the kids.

I get e-mails every now and then that say "you've made a difference in my life," which is really rewarding as a teacher. You do make a difference in their lives. It's fun to see one of your students up for a Tony, it's fun to see one of your students onstage in New York or in L.A., but they don't have to make it to New York to be successful. Many of these kids don't go into the arts at all. They become veterinarians, they go to Harvard Medical School, but the training here is phenomenal.

We teach them how to focus, how to be good managers of their time, and how to be committed. Think about the average day of an average student at OCHSA. Some of our students leave at 6:30 in the morning. They have classes, conservatory, auditions, rehearsals, and shows. They get home at 9:00 p.m. and then do their homework. That's a tough schedule for anyone, but these kids learn how to manage it and manage it well. Those skills will take them anywhere.

Interviewer: *So I hear you're pretty tough.*

Heather: I am, but the kids want to be challenged, they want to work hard. They would be disappointing themselves if they didn't work, and they know that. That's why they're here. They don't want to just come and sit and listen to you talk; they want to do the work.

Making a Difference

I always expect the best from my kids, and they disappoint me when they don't try their best. If they don't do well, it means they haven't done the work. But so many times they just go beyond what they're supposed to. There are times when they pour in so much rich emotion and give you so much from the text. On those occasions I run up and give them a hug and I get teary-eyed and then they get all emotional. It's really quite the display, but it's genuine. For me and for them that's a pay-off for going the extra mile.

Interviewer: *Does somebody stand out in your mind that really went the extra mile, did the work, faced adversity, and made a difference in their lives?*

Heather: So many of the kids have gone on to do well. I recall one young man in particular not only because of his talents and what he was able to do with them, but because of what he overcame to commit himself. He was in the ninth grade when he first auditioned for us. He didn't get in, so he auditioned the next year and did get in. He ended up getting the lead in Singing in the Rain. His dad wasn't around and his mom worked full-time as a teacher. He came to school on a skateboard. His sister was sick, and a lot of times he would have to leave early to get her medicine. He went on to do a national tour of a big tap dancing show. There were, and are, so many successes, but he stands out in my mind.

Interviewer: *What do you find most rewarding with your work here in OCHSA?*

Heather: It's rewarding to be able to make a difference in a student's life, to enrich them, to encourage them to become life-long learners, to help them to be good people. The school does that, and I think the arts do that, too. But it's a two-way street. The students enrich us and each other. They can see the violinist playing at lunch, they can see the visual artist practicing during a break, the actor working on his monologue in conservatory, and those performers are their peers. They support and respect each other's passions.

Interviewer: *If you had a potential big donor here, what would you ask them?*

Making a Difference

Heather: I would love more money. I would love to be able to offer my conservatory teachers even an hour of paid prep time. Academic teachers get a prep time. We have to make this place enticing. I would love to have the money to pay the conservatory teachers to be able to get master teachers and give them more money.

Interviewer: *What brings teachers here?*

Heather: The teachers I get in my conservatory, which is still young, we find through Ed Join and through networking. I've been in the theater for so many years and you know people and you ask people and you get people out of university.

I like to give young people with an education in the arts a chance to teach the arts. OCHSA is the best place for such teachers, because they're so passionate, they're so eager to learn. They're like sponges, the kids, and you have to match their energy. They will know if you don't know what you're talking about. These kids are smart and they want to learn and the teachers are young, but they're good.

Interviewer: *Fast-forward ten years. There are new buildings which the school owns outright. OCHSA isn't tucked away in Santa Ana, but rather celebrated on Main Street. You look back and it's been 30 years. What are you most proud of?*

Heather: The impact that I've had on the students and the enrichment that I've given them. Even today when graduates come back, they all say they were prepared for college classes. I get notes and letters from kids saying we made a difference. I just got a call from a young man that I haven't seen or talked to in three years. He said, "Even though I haven't contacted you, I want to make sure you knew you really did make a difference in my life." That's what makes me proud of OCHSA.

Portrait by Molly Esposito, Visual Arts student

What They'll Put Up With

By Lisa Novotny
Orange County High School of the Arts Parent

I almost cried the day I transferred my second child *out* of the Los Alamitos Unified School District and its conveniently located, outstanding campuses near my home so that she could join her older sister at OCHSA. With long, long lists of children desperately trying to get *into* the district, it felt totally weird to voluntarily remove both of my daughters so they could trudge to Santa Ana for a total school-involved day that runs from 6:56 a.m. (when they catch public transportation to get to school) to 6:30 p.m. (when the city bus brings them back into our area).

The schedule makes it tough for them to do anything, including homework, music lessons, etc. throughout the week. By the time they eat dinner, it's practically bedtime. You'd think with all of this, they would be clambering to get *out* of OCHSA. You'd think they would beseech me tearfully each morning to let them go to the school down the street, which would allow them to sleep in at least an hour longer, get home from school two to three hours earlier, have more play time, homework time, and sleep time. Can you think of another school for which kids would put up with all of this, let alone voluntarily demand to keep themselves tied to it? I sure can't.

But (I say, looking perplexed) these girls *want* to spend hours each day on public transportation to go to OCHSA. They don't mind getting up earlier, cramming their day into a couple of precious hours each night that are all that's left after getting to and from school and attending additional conservatory hours.

They love conservatory classes; they love those teachers who are so committed to the kids and to building their skills. They love the other kids at OCHSA who seem so open and kindhearted compared to kids almost anywhere else—kids who accept one another, who actually seem to invite differences and celebrate diversity. It's that atmosphere of acceptance and tolerance that make this whole experience valuable enough to my girls that they happily and without complaint handle logistical issues daily that most people wouldn't go through if they were *paid* to!

Miracle Worker

By Danielle Elsasser
Music and Theatre Conservatory Class of 2007

I am the best liar in the world. Ever since I can remember, I have been able to charm my way out of sticky situations. I still remember my first acting class in the sixth grade. After one semester, I knew that acting was something I wanted to do for the rest of my life. It put my wild imagination and inventive ideas to work. In eighth grade, I found out about the Orange County High School of the Arts from my acting teacher who wanted to see me take my talents to the next level. After that, my whole world changed.

My first year of conservatory was daunting, to say the least. It was a crash course on the reality of acting as a career. It forced me to grow as an individual and helped me to discover who I was and who I wanted to become. By the end of ninth grade, I realized that I wanted to use my talents to help others. Acting had changed my life, and I wanted to change the world. OCHSA gave me the opportunity to do so.

I realized exactly how I could change the world in AP biology my junior year. I had been up most of the night trying to complete the eight hours of homework that my teacher had assigned. I was exhausted, stressed, and at the end of my rope, but I was happy. After half a year of the hardest class I had ever taken, I knew that I wanted to be a pediatrician. My best friend was suspicious of my newfound life goal. I had changed my career path several times before, but this, I knew, was it.

Doctors have to save lives physically, but they have the ability to rebuild lives emotionally. With my love of science and my acting talents, I know that I can do both. When faced with the seriousness of a patient's illness or disability, I will have to put on a strong face no matter what the odds. My theatrical background will help me give patients hope, and hope can work miracles.

Dreams Inspire Dreamers to Bigger Dreams

An Interview with Kate Peters
Gala 2007 "Masterpiece in the Making" Chair

Alee was a talented musician from an early age. She loved the viola and she loved the bass, and she's played them since she was in fourth grade. At some point it became obvious that what she needed was the kind of education that would foster her talents, give her lots of opportunity to not only play those instruments but to develop her entire portfolio of musical skills.

She even brought it up to us. She said, "What about OCHSA?" We were looking at all the options for schools. The thing that amazed me was that OCHSA was also an exceptionally fine academic school. I didn't know that. I had watched OCHSA from the time it was born, knowing that it was a high school of the arts—a good high school for the arts—but not really knowing how good it was academically.

So we created a spreadsheet of all the schools that were possible for her to attend that made sense. When we entered the information for the schools, evaluating the arts education, the academic performance, the test score results, the percentage of students that went on to college, and the school ranking in county, state, and district. In the final analysis, we found that OCHSA was far above the schools in our district. The fact that Allie's interests were in the arts made OCHSA stand out all the more. It was absolutely the best place for her.

And then Allie surprised us. She changed her mind and was fairly resistant to going to OCHSA, even though originally she had been the one to say, "Well, let's consider OCHSA." When it came down to the time to actually make the choice, she wasn't sure if she wanted to do it. She had a lot of close friends who were not going to OCHSA.

OCHSA is a unique environment. Not everybody is going to feel comfortable there, but I think that a lot of young people do come here because they feel like it's a place where they finally fit in. That wasn't our case. Our daughter had lots of friends and enjoyed being where she was. However, one of the most important things that she learned during her first year at OCHSA was that if she was going to succeed, it was up to her. It was tough for her. Although she may feel that her drive has always been a part of who she is, which I somewhat agree with, I think at some point she was encouraged to make a decision and to say, "Are you going to be doing this for you or for someone else? And if you're doing it for you, what do you want to do, what do you really want to do? Where do you really want to go with your life let alone today?" She

Dreams Inspire Dreamers to Bigger Dreams

chose to continue at OCHSA. Now she is better academically and musically—and she knows it. She knows she's grown, and she knows she will continue to grow even though some of her closest friends are still not at OCHSA.

I think one of the most important factors in Allie deciding to stay at OCHSA and doing so well at the school has been the faculty, and particularly the conservatory faculty. These are professionals who are some of the best in the country, certainly the best in the state; these are people whom she respects because of who they are and what they do; and these are teachers who are nurturing but don't put up with complaining and whining. I think encouragement without babying is something she understands and respects. It's something that will teach her what she needs to understand to succeed in performing and in living.

One of the things that I love about OCHSA is that it encourages young people to dream big. I think that comes from the fact that OCHSA was a big dream itself, and continues to be. That dream is coming true and the young people feel it, they see it, they're part of it. So what I've seen, for example, is my daughter doesn't just talk about going to college, she talks about going to college, learning culinary skills, opening/buying a hotel, opening a restaurant in the hotel, a chain of hotels,

a chain of restaurants—it goes on and on. Now as a young person, she may decide the next day that it's not hotels, it's something else, but I don't see her dreams being small anymore. I see them being as large as OCHSA's dreams, and that's because dreams spawn more dreams.

Big dreams spawn other big dreams. Students from OCHSA have gone on to become stars on Broadway and brain surgeons in renowned hospitals. They participate in many aspects of life in big ways, and they encourage other people to do the same wherever they are. The impact that OCHSA has is not only on the students, faculty, parents, and families who are part of OCHSA but on the community, the entire county, the state, even the nation, maybe the world.

The Drama of Life

An Interview with Kristin Gilmore
Music and Theatre Conservatory Class of 1998

When I was at OCHSA (and Los Alamitos High School), I applied to colleges both in theater and in international relations because at the time I thought I had two divergent loves. It turns out, however, that international relations and drama are closely intertwined, as my own experiences and the current political situation will certainly attest.

No doubt, OCHSA helped me get into Carnegie Mellon. I started studying English at Carnegie Mellon so I could keep up my study of the theater and my study of drama through the study of literature. Then, I had the opportunity my junior year to study abroad in South Africa. I fell in love with the African continent and decided that I wanted to pursue international relations. After my senior year, I applied to Yale University for graduate school in international relations with a concentration on the African continent. I was accepted at Yale and spent two years in a graduate program at there.

At OCHSA, our program was diverse. The students came from all parts of Orange County, and I was able to meet students whom I would not have been able to meet had I gone to the high school in my local district. Having been able to meet people from different backgrounds, cultures, and strata of life opened my eyes and instilled in me a desire and need to meet new and interesting people. In this way, OCHSA inspired my study of international relations. My experiences there continue to help me manage my intercultural interactions when I'm abroad.

It was my second year at Yale when I was contacted by my alma mater, Carnegie Mellon University, about opening a branch campus in the Middle East, in Qatar. I knew where Qatar was and, of course, I was flattered that Carnegie Mellon had thought of me to work for them overseas as part of the student affairs operation. I wasn't studying student affairs per se when I took the job in Qatar, but being a broadly educated individual, something that I had started to become while I was a student at OCHSA, enabled me to take the job and to be successful working in the Middle East for over two years.

In the music and theatre program at OCHSA, you learn to think on your feet. Our first classes our freshman year were about improvisation. I feel like we spent the entire first year doing improv. Undoubtedly, when you're living abroad, you need to think on your feet quickly to adapt to local environments and circumstances. Living in the Middle East especially, there were some tenuous situations which warranted quick adaptation. For example, there was a bombing the first March that I was there. As campus administrators we had to figure out what we were going to do with our students the following day. How were we going to talk about the bombing in a context of most of the staff being American and the attacks being targeted against Americans and other foreign

The Drama of Life

nationals? How were we going to interchange and dialogue with our Middle Eastern students? The confidence I gained through doing improvisation, as silly as that may sound, was something I drew on in that situation. I also drew on my public speaking skills, which I was confident about having made good use of those skills garnered during my time at OCHSA.

After the bombing, we sat down with the students and had a "talk shop." We talked through all of the issues and emotions students were dealing with as a result of the bombing, because in actuality Qatar is a very safe place. They had never had an attack like that on Qatari soil before. So, we started talking about some of those issues. We started from the base level of "I'm scared, I'm wondering if this is going to happen again, I'm afraid I'm going to be the target of attack." We then looked at the current political situation and talked about some interactions with literature. For example, we brought in Edward Said. We engaged them in a broad-based level of discussion so they could talk about the bombing within an academic framework. Ultimately, there was the sense that we were accomplishing our mission as an academic institution, but also dealing with the real human emotions and problems that the students were having in response to the attack.

Around this time, I did think about leaving, but more often I thought about staying—about what I could do and what I could contribute if I stayed. I worried more about my family worrying about me than I worried about my own safety, because I knew that the friends and connections I had made in the Middle East would help me get through that difficult time.

I don't act at all anymore, but I certainly direct. My official position at Carnegie Mellon University was Director of Student Activities. At OCHSA, I was a student director in music and theatre starting my sophomore year. In fact, my senior year I was given free reign to direct my own full-scale production. I directed A. R. Gurney's "The Dining Room" all by myself. I did the dramaturgy. I found the sets at garage sales. I got the costumes together out of my parents' closet, ran rehearsals at my house, put together the program, and did all my own advertising, in addition to casting the play, directing my actors, and seeing through my vision of doing my own production. It was a challenging, but rewarding experience that yielded valuable lessons, many of which I utilize today in everyday life to manage my own schedule and my many commitments. In directing, you get to be involved in the conceptual part of the play— to be involved in decision making and processing. Directing has inspired me to think more broadly about my life and my part in the world.

Landscape by Nicole Ahn, Visual Arts student

For the Roses Had the Look of Flowers that are Looked At

By Heather Gibbs
Music and Theatre Class of 2007

Orange County High School of the Arts. OCHSA. The greatest place on Earth. The most amazing high school in the history of mankind. I have been bestowed with the special honor of attending this prestigious school for all four years of my high school career. This magnificent art institute helps you realize and reach all of your wildest dreams. Anything that you can imagine, you can achieve when you attend OCHSA.

Before I won the knowledge lottery, I was winning the stupidity raffle, taking home the grand prize in ugly, and getting Nobel Prizes for my surplusage of fat. I was a loner; lonesome and alone in my misery. If I was fortunate enough to have someone speak to me, I would immediately freeze up and saliva would start running down my chin. I was a mess; extremely unkempt with the haunting aroma of burning hair that seemed doomed to halo around my cranium for nothing short of an eternity. The smell was of such intensity that even my family refused to speak to me. It would appear to be my fate to wander the Earth forever with no friends, no brain, no heart, and no courage. This all changed when the much acclaimed OCHSA opened her loving heart and clasped me to her bosom, accepting me, flaws and all.

OCHSA took the place of my family that had abandoned me while pursuing their feeble attempt to get me to shower. OCHSA was my mother, my father—giving me support, letting me know that I could achieve anything that I could think up. OCHSA cleansed me and washed away my dowdiness, replacing my shabby dress with garments only a queen would wear, my curly burned hair with pure spun gold. My empty cobweb-filled head was given a brain equivalent to that of Einstein and Da Vinci combined. I excelled in all my academic classes and at the end of each year had no less that a 10.5 GPA, superseding that of any other student, ever.

Not only was I proficient in my academic classes, but I exceeded everyone's expectations outside of school as well. Since being warmly welcomed into the OCHSA family, I have scaled Mount Everest twice in the past two months, ridden atop a hammerhead shark, and discovered the lost City of Atlantis. I have also discovered life on Mars. I set up an alliance with the Martians, and they now provide us with unlimited natural resources. A month ago I had a long talk first with God, and then Satan. I successfully settled the bitter resentment between them. I discovered the meaning of life and wrote it down on a piece of paper. Unfortunately, I used that same piece of paper to write down the cure to cancer and both the secret and the cure are no longer legible. I have completed many minor accomplishments similar to the ones already listed, and I am well on my way to another successful year.

OCHSA can help you do anything you want and much more than you could ever dream. Everybody who is lost, suffering, and alone in the world needs to flock to OCHSA. There they will discover what life is all about, they will discover the perfect recipe for life, love, laughter, hope, and a healthy dose of human compassion.

THE CONCLUSION

"*There is a time for many words, and there is also a time to sleep.*"

--THE ODYSSEY, HOMER

Unfolding

By Buck Minister Fullerine
Orange County High School of the Arts Founder

Fourteen whistles to the wind, you pipe your sails—slow, taking in that last breath before you say "damn it all to hell," of course, and pull the wheel round bout. Out here where it's strange and blue and your talk is stage plays, you decide to relax and enjoy your unfolding.

Some would grow up and say, "I did something," but you'll hear a quote that'll put in your place of warm understanding. That's a sweet rush and suddenly your life can be flat as paper. You've found the others, a clean plane that comes at you and you can read the grain like an old tree.

...and your map unfolds, the dots connect, and you're just left thanking the sailors that have led you to these seas. We've more paper airplanes to create.

About the Orange County High School of the Arts

SCHOOL OVERVIEW

As one of the premier arts schools in the nation, the Orange County High School of the Arts embraces and encourages artistic creativity and academic excellence. This innovative public charter school provides a uniquely challenging and nurturing environment focused on individual growth, opportunity, and diversity. The U.S. Department of Education and the National Endowment for the Arts have recognized the Orange County High School of the Arts as a model arts education program. The school is also accredited by the Western Association of Schools and Colleges (WASC).

STUDENTS AND FACULTY

The school currently serves a culturally diverse student body of more than 1,300 students from 92 cities throughout Southern California in grades 7-12. The academic faculty is fully credentialed, and the majority of the 200 arts and academic teachers hold advanced degrees. They are dedicated and supportive professionals who help students develop the skills necessary to succeed in higher education, or a profession in the arts. Guest artists and industry leaders also share their expertise and creativity with students through lectures, presentations, and hands-on training.

CURRICULUM

Academics: The Orange County High School of the Arts provides a rigorous academic program aligned to the California State Standards. Students attend approximately five hours of academic classes in addition to three hours of daily arts instruction. Students maintain a school-wide Grade Point Average (GPA) of 3.23, with the senior class averaging a 3.21 GPA. More than ten percent of the junior and senior classes earn a 4.0 GPA or higher. The school also offers thirteen Advanced Placement classes.

Offering one of the most demanding and intensive academic programs in Southern California, the school has been ranked in the top ten percent of high schools in the State of California, and is one of the top five highest ranking high school academic programs in Orange County, based on an Academic Performance Index (API) test score of 870. In 2005, the Orange County High School of the Arts was the only school in Orange County with 100% of its students to pass the California High School Exit Exam (CAHSEE).

Arts: Now celebrating its 20th year, the Orange County High School of the Arts is the place for aspiring young artists to refine their skills and flourish in one of 11 arts conservatories offered, including Ballet Folklorico, Classical & Contemporary Dance, Commercial Dance, Creative Writing, Film & Television, Instrumental Music, Integrated Arts, Music & Theatre, Opera, Production & Design, or Visual Arts.

About the Orange County High School of the Arts

COLLEGE ACCEPTANCE

Ninety-eight percent of the school's graduates are accepted into institutions of higher education and the remaining pursue a career in the arts industry upon graduation.

ADMISSION REQUIREMENTS

Interested applicants must have a minimum of a 2.0 GPA and satisfactory citizenship. All applicants must audition and provide transcripts and letters of recommendation.

TUITION

The school is tuition free, donation dependent. No student is admitted or denied based on financial capacity.

FUNDING

The 2006-2007 school year is based on a $12 million total operating budget. Academic instruction is funded by the State of California, totaling $8 million. The school relies solely on the generosity of individual donors, the business community, and foundations to fund the 11 pre-professional arts conservatories. The school must raise more than $4 million this year — approximately $2,500 per student — to continue offering a comprehensive arts program. Nearly 25% of the school's 1,300 students have requested financial assistance to help fund their arts conservatory program.

PARTNERSHIPS

The Orange County High School of the Arts has built partnerships with institutions of higher education and professional arts organizations, including:

> American Ballet Intensives
> Chapman University
> Los Angeles Philharmonic
> Opera Pacific
> Orange County Performing Arts Center
> Pacific Symphony
> Philharmonic Society of Orange County
> South Coast Repertory
> University of California, Irvine
> Vanguard University

About the Orange County High School of the Arts

CALIFORNIA ARTS CENTER (CAC)

Whether expressed with the flourish of a paintbrush, a leap through the air or in the passion of a monologue, there's no denying the amazing effect the arts can have on a person. The California ARTS Center (CAC) provides a variety of arts programs for children and adults who are interested in exploring the arts. CAC provides students of all socio and economic levels with an opportunity to explore a wider range of art curriculums and to participate in a unique educational experience. CAC offers evening, weekend and summer classes for children and adults.

COMMUNITY OUTREACH

Camp OCHSA is a FREE interactive arts training workshop available to students in grades 4-6 residing or attending school in Santa Ana, CA. The program offers classes in dance, drama, vocal music, and visual arts and introduces young people to the basic language, techniques, and skills in their chosen area of study.

For additional information about California Arts Center, Camp OCHSA and to enroll, please contact Pat McMaster at (714) 560-0900 Ext. 5630 or pat.mcmaster@ocsarts.net.

AWARDS & SPECIAL RECOGNITION

No Child Left Behind – Blue Ribbon School (U.S. Department of Education), 2006

International NETWORK of Schools for the Advancement of Arts Education's 2006 Exemplary School Award recipient

California Distinguished School (California Department of Education), 2005

Creative Ticket National School of Distinction Award (Kennedy Center Alliance for Arts Education Network and the California Alliance for Arts Education), 2005

Only accredited operatic producing high school in the nation recognized by Opera America, 2004

American Society of Composers, Authors, and Publishers Award for Adventurous Programming of Contemporary Music, 1999-2004

About the Orange County High School of the Arts

STAR School Award presented by The International NETWORK of Performing and Visual Arts Schools, 2001

Model Arts Education Program (California Department of Education), 1998

National Blue Ribbon School Award with Special Honors in Arts Education (National Endowment for the Arts and the U.S. Department of Education), 1998

Annual Golden Bell Award (California School Board Association), 1996

McDonnell Douglas Crystal Vision Award, 1996

Disney Community Service Award, 1995

LOCATION
The campus is centrally located in Santa Ana, the heart of Orange County at:
1010 N. Main Street, Santa Ana, CA 92701
Phone: 714.560.0900
Fax: 714.664.0463
www.ocsarts.net

www.ingramcontent.com/pod-product-compliance
Lightning Source LLC
Chambersburg PA
CBHW080731020726
47503CB00010B/2875